Time To Be Free

Marcia Aka-Kadjo

Time To Be Free by Marcia Aka-Kadjo

ISBN- 978 -0-9956940-1-9

Cover by William Hunter, hunterdesign@live.com

CONTENTS

ACKNOWLEDGEMENTS

I would like to thank all of my friends and family for being supportive, and encouraging me to complete this book. A special thank you to Uche Nnoka, Neala Okuramade, Nichola Williams, Janet Dorling and Jason Douglas for their suggestions on ways to improve and complete this book. William Hunter, thank you for being able to translate what was in my head and on my heart, the book cover is beautiful.

To my dear pastor and spiritual mother Pastor Sheron Ankrah. I would like to express my gratitude for your love, input, direction, prayers and wisdom.

Pastors Joseph Boadu and Philip Ankrah, I would like to say a special thank you for the many years of input and wise counsel and for being men of integrity. You and all of the Pastors at Christian Life Fellowship are a great example to us.

Thank you to Peter Horrobin and his teams at Ellel Ministries, your ministry has been, and continues to be, such a blessing.

I would like to thank my loving husband Jean-Marc and our children Julienne, Jesse and Alexander. You have kept me going when I felt like giving up, constantly reminding me of the bigger picture. I love you all very much. Thank you for your love, patience and encouragement…it is finished!

The one I must thank the most is my Abba, my Father, my God. He continues to prove to me that with Him all things are possible and for this He deserves all the thanks, all the glory and continuous praise.

INTRODUCTION

Over the years people have suggested that I share my story to testify of the hope, healing and restorative power of God. It has been a long journey, but I thank God for His faithfulness and bringing me this far.

Most of us have been in battles, and some of us have been through what seems like a war, during which we have been injured and scarred. Some of us are still nursing our wounds, holding onto them even though Jesus died so that we can live an abundant life, free from all of the aforementioned. Through Jesus we have been given the cure – the antidote – and upon accepting Jesus as our Lord and saviour, we also accept Him as our healer. It's not just a beautiful song to sing on Saturdays or Sundays, or whenever our church services are held.

As the body of Christ our healing, our deliverance, our restoration is in Him and through Him, they are all given to us freely by Him.

When I gave my life to the Lord I allowed Him to heal most areas, but there were particular things I held onto, certain areas I wouldn't allow Him to have access to. I had no idea why, but I just couldn't seem to let them go.

It wasn't until 12 years later that I understood why I had held on to the very things that were causing me pain, disturbing me and tormenting me. I was going around in circles. I would feel free, unburdened and victorious one minute and then the next minute something would happen, such as a disagreement with someone in church or my husband, a challenge with ministry, finances or work, and I would retreat in offence or fear. For years I didn't understand why I couldn't seem to overcome and be consistently free from the things that held me captive. I'm still a work in progress, but I'd like to share my story so far.

My hope is that as you read you'll see that if Jesus can heal and restore me, He can do the same for you, too. As He reveals Himself to you, I hope that you will allow Him to show you the truth about who He created you to be.

I am grateful for your restoration, thankful for your freedom and excited about the plans and purpose He has for you! I pray that His will above all else will be established in your lives.

It's time to begin.

CHAPTER ONE

A Life-changing Moment

I remember it like it was yesterday, because there are some moments in life that you just never forget.

I left the office, said goodbye to my gastroenterologist's secretary, walked down the stairs and made my way out of the hospital. I remember opting for the stairs, as the lift would have meant being around people, and I wanted to be alone to try and digest what I had heard. The steps I took to get to the station seemed like thousands, even though that was impossible as the station was only a stone's through away from the hospital. I stood outside London Bridge station and gazed over at the hospital with my mind a blur. I had mentioned to friends of mine in jest that I sensed 2001 was going to be an eventful year, but little did I know that this was now becoming a self-fulfilling prophecy.

My brother Wayne had asked me to call him once I had received the results of the tests. My family had journeyed with me since my return from Egypt in November 2000. This part of the journey was not as scenic and pleasurable, but Wayne had been there every step of the way: I needed to tell him.

"Wayne, it's me," I said.

"Hiya sis, you alright? How did it go with the consultant?"

"I'm outside the station now, but I need to get back to work," I said, delaying the moment I would have to break the news. "I just wanted to give you a call quickly before I get on the tube."

"Okay. So, what were the results?"

I didn't know how to tell my brother. I didn't want him to feel he was responsible for me yet again, as he had been there for me unconditionally throughout my life and needed to get on with his own. He and his fiancée Elaine were planning their wedding and were to be married that year. The last thing I wanted was to be a burden to them leading up to their special day.

"Well, I sensed something was wrong, but I didn't expect this."Mars, what's going on, what are you talking about? You don't sound right. Talk to me, Mars." The reality began to hit and I began to cry. "Wayne, I have cancer, they found cancer." I broke down and cried like a baby in the middle of the street. Passers-by watched me as I went into meltdown. "Mars, everything is going to be okay, I'm coming down. Tell me when you need me to be down and I'll be there."

I was booked in to see the surgeon the following day and explained that to Wayne.

"Okay, we'll be down tonight. Don't worry, everything is going to be just fine."

I realised at that point that Elaine would be coming down from Sheffield too. Wayne also needed moral support.

I felt as though my whole world was falling apart.

I had to get my act together and regain my composure. I needed to let it all out, but London Bridge Station wasn't the time or the place. I told myself that I was fine and needed to get on with things and go back to work.

I said goodbye to Wayne and looked forward to seeing him later that evening.

I knew that alone, behind closed doors, was the time that I would be more vulnerable. I was grateful that I had such a caring brother, who was willing to drop everything to be with me at such a challenging time.

I don't remember how long it took for me to get back to work and I don't remember going up to the restaurant with my manager. I do remember sitting opposite her and telling her the results of the many months of tests that I had undertaken. I left her in the restaurant that day with clear instructions of what to say to those who questioned my absence, an absence that turned out to be 15 months long. The process had begun.

CHAPTER TWO

Preparing For Battle

Up until that point I had never been seriously ill; no regular colds, no sickness, nothing broken or sprained. The whole situation was quite overwhelming: I was about to go from a fit and active life – running a few miles and working out in the gym about five times a week – to knocking on death's door overnight, without warning. I couldn't get my head around it.

Wayne and Elaine came to London from Sheffield that night as promised and we went to visit the surgeon. Speaking to him made me a little more peaceful, but I was not completely at ease. The surgeon's priority was to make sure I understood the procedure I would be going through but my thoughts were dominated by the question, "What if something happens in theatre and I don't come out from being under the anaesthetic?"

I couldn't get this thought out of my mind. The strange thing was that I was much more afraid of the operation at that stage than of the cancer. I felt that something bad was going to happen.

My second major concern was the position of the scar. The surgeon mentioned that as I was young it was probably best if I had a scar around my bikini line and that the incision ought to be as small as possible. It sounded good to me: I still wanted to be able to wear a bikini, but didn't want to have a scar so large that people would stare and begin to ask me questions.

The surgery was scheduled for the following week, Wednesday 7 February at 10 am. This gave me time to sort everything and everyone out.

Wayne was already suggesting that I go to Sheffield and stay with him and Elaine after the operation, but I wanted to stay in my flat in London, as I really didn't want to be a burden to anyone. I would work something out.

The day of the surgery arrived very quickly. I had been off work since my consultant had broken the news to me the previous week and, having more time on my hands than usual, I had spent a lot of time in prayer. It was funny to me that I was praying, not really caring whether my prayers were being heard. I didn't even know what I believed in, really, I prayed to Jesus because I truly believed that all roads of faith lead to Him. That gave me some kind of release, but I knew that alone wasn't enough. I had to do something too: make a battle plan.

I needed to be clear how I would attack the disease. It had invaded my body without my consent and I was not happy about that at all. I suppose that was the practical side of me taking over. I would always say, "Everything has a place and every place has a thing."

In my mind, it was all about order. This disease was no different to the way I organised everything in my life, and my approach towards cancer would be the same. I needed to bring order and balance back to my body as the disease seemed completely chaotic and unpredictable. Regardless of this rollercoaster, I wanted to feel well again. The first thing was to have the operation and get rid of what was causing me to have the excruciating stomach pains I had been suffering from for about two years. After that I would do whatever was necessary to be one 100 per cent fit and well again.

Wayne and Elaine had returned to Sheffield shortly after the meeting with the surgeon, but Wayne promised me he would be back in London the evening before the surgery was scheduled to take place as he wanted to be with me throughout the operation.

Operation day arrived, and Wayne was with me as promised. I was glad that out of all of my family members it was Wayne who was with me, as he was able to make any situation appear funny and positive; he was like a ray of sunshine on a cloudy day. It sounded corny, but he was. Only he could make me laugh or take the mickey out of me when I was just about to be sliced open. Only Wayne. That was the beauty of my brother – his ability to see the brighter and lighter side of things no matter what the circumstances.

I remember being very nervous before going down to theatre. I was truly like a duck in water, gliding on the surface, but paddling like crazy beneath. I had never really been able to show my true feelings, especially in dire circumstances, as I was always concerned about how my emotion would affect others. I had carried so much for so long, and as I was about to enter theatre I was petrified, but at the same time there was a sense of relief. I couldn't explain it, but there was a little voice in my head saying, "Well, you haven't lived such a bad life and if you don't make it back, then at least you have helped the people around you. You're not such a horrible person, you could have achieved more, but never mind."

I began to see events in my life flash before me and many thoughts ran through my mind. I thought about what I could have done, what I should have done and what I should have said to particular individuals. I thought of all the 'could haves', 'should haves' and 'maybes', and they played like a film in my mind. Wayne saw my countenance changing.

"Mars, are you alright?"

At that point I wondered whether to lie or not.

"Wayne, if I don't make it out I've left the flat to you and the girls. Please make sure that they don't waste the money and that they do something constructive with it, okay?"

Wayne looked at me and put on his authoritarian voice. "Sis, I don't want to hear you speaking like that at all. If you go in there with that attitude you might not make it back out. Think of all of the things you have to live for. I love you and so do many other people. I won't have you speaking to me about not coming out … even though I've always liked your flat." Wayne was grinning with that big, white-toothed smile of his, as cheeky and infectious as ever. He made me think about the things that I wanted to live for. Right at this moment the list was short, but I wasn't sure when faced with death, whether I wanted to die either.

It was time. The porters came to collect me to go down to theatre, and Wayne walked as far as he could with me. He held my hand tightly before having to let go. As he looked at me with glistening, apprehensive eyes he mouthed, "It's going to be alright."

I gave him a half-hearted smile because at that moment I had never felt so vulnerable. I was the one who always helped others, who encouraged them, who built them up, who was the shoulder to cry on, and now I felt of no use to anyone, not even myself.

CHAPTER THREE

The Battle For Life

I tried to move, but my body was unable to go to where I directed it, I felt weak and very tired. I remembered what I had said to God before I went in for surgery: "If you are real and can hear me, please let me live." If He let me live I would go to church and be a good girl.

There must have been a God because I was still alive. I was thankful and felt as though it was a new beginning for me – that I had been given a second chance at life. I wanted to get up and shout from the rooftops, but the most I could do was move my head a little as the wound hurt so much when I moved even the slightest. Wayne was there at my bedside.

"They said that I can't make you laugh because of your stitches, but I'm still deliberating." That was Wayne, who didn't bother with the conventional "Hello" and was just as cheeky as ever. I smiled and the smile was about to turn into a laugh, but then I felt the pain hit me and I changed my mind quickly. "Wayne, it hurts, so please don't make me laugh," I pleaded with him.

"Aw sis, that's no fun is it? I'll have to think about it."

All I could think was, "That boy!"

Two days had gone by without me even realising. It was Friday and I still felt as though I had just come back from theatre. The morphine must have taken its toll on my system, as I was really out of it. The surgery had gone well, I was told. The nurse came to check that I wasn't in extreme pain and to show me how to use the morphine machine. I was one who would normally choose to abstain from drugs, medical and otherwise, but the morphine was much appreciated! I had a drip, a catheter, the morphine machine and the oxygen pipe attached to my nose. All of that plus my sexy surgery socks, it was all too much to take in. Wayne could see that I was overwhelmed and tried to distract me with humour, his usual weapon.

I was still very dazed as the morphine left me quite light-headed, to the point where I couldn't really co-ordinate my movements. People had always told me that I was always on the go and that at times I just need to 'keep my backside quiet'. Well, now quiet had been forced upon me and I had no choice in the matter.

The surgeon was straight to the point and professional when he arrived at my bedside, but at the same time I felt that he actually cared about me, and that I wasn't just another case for him. He had asked to be contacted when I came around so that he could speak to me. I thought that was considerate of him. He explained that the troublemaker was a tumour the size of my fist that had been attached to my bladder and uterus. The surgery had taken a little longer than expected because the tumour was bleeding and causing obstruction. He explained that my spleen had also been removed and the results had shown that the tumour was cancerous, but my spleen was not.

He had also taken samples of the walls of the uterus, bladder and spleen to check to see if the cancer had penetrated any of their walls. All seemed clear. He also explained that he had removed the part of my bowel where the polyps were (they called it a hemi-colectomy) and removed a little more of the bowel at either side of the polyps just to be safe. He explained that usually this procedure would call for the patient to have a colostomy bag in order for the fluid to be constantly drained from the bowel, but due to my age he had tried his best not to do that. Instead he re-joined the bowel – literally sewed it back together – so that I could have a normal life once everything healed. I didn't really understand what he was saying at the time, I was just thankful.

The polyps were what my gastroenterologist had recommended surgery for, as the test results had shown them to be cancerous, but I don't think that the surgeon expected to find so much going on when he opened me up. I thanked God for such a meticulous and talented surgeon. God really seemed to put the right people in place for me.

I had begun to digest all of the information that was filtering through Wayne to me. We were told that the source of my stomach cramps was the tumour, and it all began to make sense. Around the time of my monthly cycle the pain would become unbearable, and I would sometimes just stay in bed for a few days until the pain subsided. I had quite a high pain threshold, but the pain was excruciating and would hit me at the most inconvenient times, like when I was about to sign a client in at work! I remember an occasion when I had to signal to my colleagues to take over while I gripped the desk until the spasm ended. It was not only painful, but it was extremely embarrassing. The pieces of the puzzle were beginning to be put in place and were becoming much clearer.

As I began to think about being discharged from hospital, I was given a list of things I needed to refrain from doing by the physiotherapist and nurses at home. I was told that these guidelines were to help with my recuperation over the months that followed. In order for my wound to heal well and prevent any complications, they suggested I adhere to the instructions completely. I was advised not to lift anything heavy, not even a kettle, for a month or so. That sounded absolutely absurd to me. I was told that as things began to heal on the outside that it may seem okay to do things such as lifting, but I needed to remember that the wound had to heal on the inside. I had gone through major surgery and there were also several organs that needed to heal. I listened, but in my mind I always had a better plan and my own goals. If they said to me that I would be on the mend and ready to go in three months then I would set a goal of six to eight weeks; that was just the way I was.

When the surgeon left the room, Wayne told me that he and Elaine were preparing their spare bedroom for me, as they thought it wouldn't be wise for me to stay alone in the flat. "You can always go back to the flat once you're feeling a bit stronger and able to cope on your own." Wayne said.

I realised that I didn't really have any choice but to be reliant on my family members at that stage. I didn't particularly like the idea, but I was in a bit of a sticky situation and didn't have the energy to argue or state my case, so I went along with their plans.

The days that followed in the hospital were slow and tiresome. I did very little, yet felt as though I had been to the gym, worked through the day and partied all night. It was strange how I felt exhausted while doing nothing. I put it down to the drugs. On the eighth day, they removed the last of my attachments, the catheter. They had been removing the tubes one by one; first the oxygen pipe in my nose, then the morphine line and now it was time to deal with the catheter. It had been sewn in, so there was a small procedure to remove the stitches and then it was out. I felt free at last. I hadn't been able to venture further than my room for eight days and was unable to take a shower, but had managed to wash myself.

These early days after my surgery were reminiscent of the days I spent in St Thomas' Hospital on my return from Egypt. I had contracted salmonella and shigella and was too weak to even stand, so Mum would wash me down in bed. Not being able to do things for myself because of limited movement and energy was a very humbling experience and both times that it happened to me I was very aware of what life must be like for the elderly. I felt sorry for those who were co-dependent; I knew it must be such a degrading experience for them. Relieved that my time of confinement was limited, unlike them, was what enabled me to cope and remain positive.

Once I was pipe-free I was able to begin physiotherapy. It seemed ridiculous that walking around the ward, a 50 to 100-metre stretch, was my challenge for the day. I would normally have completed that in about 30 seconds flat, but now it took me about nearly 10 minutes, as I could only manage to take small steps. As I walked I held my wound, as when I stood up it felt as though it was about to split open and spill my stomach onto the floor. It was then that I realised that it may take me a little longer to heal than I expected. Any movement brought agony.

The last days of physiotherapy, and the cracker diet to help my colon to begin to work again, were helpful and prepared me nicely for my release from hospital. The oncologist that I had been referred to by my surgeon popped into my room to see me the day before I was due to be discharged. He seemed like an interesting character, a no-nonsense kind of man. The oncologist felt my tummy firmly, looked at the scar and came to the conclusion that I ought to have a break for a few weeks and then begin chemotherapy. He wanted to begin chemotherapy sessions promptly due to my age, and he wanted to ensure that everything cancerous was destroyed so that I could have the best possible chance of survival. I was a bit stunned because I thought he would have allowed more time for the wound to heal, but he seemed to know what he was talking about, so I went along with what he suggested.

The time had arrived for me to leave London Bridge hospital. The 10 days there had been a blur, and there was still much progress to be made in terms of internal healing, but I was pleased to be leaving the place, even if it was just for a few weeks reprieve. My stomach had begun to work again, but still could only tolerate bland, basic foods. The first thing that I had tried to eat a few days after surgery was a cracker, and that didn't stay in my system very long. It was then that I realised that it would be a slow and gruelling process to recovery, and maybe not at the pace I was used to working at. I was discharged from the hospital. I was able to drink a little bit of water; crackers and foods that were dry and light seemed to make my stomach happy I felt like a baby – I hadn't realised that the operation would have had such an effect.

I was going to be in Yorkshire with Wayne and Elaine until my chemotherapy ended and I was stronger and able to cope with taking care of myself. I was quite apprehensive on the one hand and extremely grateful on the other because I knew that I wouldn't have been able to care for myself. My cousin Danny collected me from the hospital, as Wayne was at work. It was really kind of him to drive all the way from Sheffield. I was seeing so many random acts of kindness that showed me just how gorgeous the people around me were, and it made me appreciate them all the more.

The journey back to Sheffield was quite arduous; I thanked God for the person who had come up with the idea of service stations! I had a pillow in the back of the car and tried to lie as flat as possible, as sitting up straight put more pressure on my wound and was quite painful. The journey seemed longer than usual, probably because we kept stopping in order for me to stretch and not become too uncomfortable, but we got there in the end.

I didn't think that I would be happy to be in Yorkshire. I expected to miss my London life, but it turned out to be quite a joyful experience.

Wayne would carry me down from my bedroom to the living room first thing in the morning. I could only walk short distances as walking up and down the stairs put extra strain on my wound. The days began at about seven o'clock in the morning when I would lay on the sofa watching television and falling in and out of sleep. I couldn't concentrate enough to read as the pain relief kept me dazed and confused, so I slept as much as I could and took pleasure in it, knowing that as I slept my body was healing and repairing itself. I would wander into the kitchen, hobbling like someone three times my age, to get some water. It worked in my favour that my body wasn't tolerating much food, and I would nibble on a cracker or two until Wayne and Elaine returned home at about five o'clock in the evening.

Mum lived about an hour and a half away from Wayne, and she would come to Sheffield for a few days when she could. The fear that I would be a burden to my family was one of the main reasons that I didn't want to go to Yorkshire to recuperate in the first place; I didn't want to bother anyone. If I had stayed in London my friends would have been great, but their work commitments meant that their lives were full enough already; I couldn't have asked them to help me. I was reluctant to expect that of my family either – I didn't want to put them in a position whereby they felt obliged to take care of me, and I didn't want the arguments that went with it all. Up to now my philosophy had been that everyone was busy and had their lives to get on with. It would grieve me sometimes that some of my family were slow to react when I needed help, yet I was always there for them at the drop of a hat. I had concluded that it was best not to focus too much on my family, but accept that no family was perfect.

I enjoyed being by myself because I'd realised that people didn't actually know what to say to me, so there was always an awkward silence in place of normal conversation. The last thing that I wanted was for people to feel uncomfortable, so rather than have that I told them that I was fine during the day on my own as I was resting. That way they didn't feel guilty and I didn't feel burdened, it was the best solution all round.

I had plenty of time to think. It seemed that for most of my life I had taken care of others; my Mum, from the age of eight when she had begun drinking; my niece, from the age of 10, when my sister gave birth to her as a teenager and she lived in our house; my sister's other children as they came along and she needed help in raising them; my friends as they needed help and direction; and the men who I had been involved with who seemed to need stability and a mother figure in their lives.

I was a care-taker, the mothering type. I didn't realise that I had assumed that role from the age of eight and never let go of it. I had not allowed anyone to take care of me, possibly because I had been let down, abandoned and rejected on many an occasion. As a result of that I would not trust anyone to take care of me. That also explained the obsessive, controlling behaviour I displayed when I wanted to do everything by myself and would not allow people to help me to complete the smallest of tasks. I thought about all of the situations and people that I had come across, and had been involved with in one way or another, and the reality of just how much I had controlled my existence. I had never let anyone into my world completely, not even my family. It had taken me 20 years to form a cocoon that was a safe place where I could survive. The question was, did I need to continue to live a cocooned existence in order to survive? It was quite ironic: I had been fiercely protecting myself and forming a safe external space in which to live and survive, while internally I was dying. I had thought I had everything covered.

CHAPTER FOUR

Retreat, Recover, Research

Chemo began on 27 February 2001 and was something that I could quite easily have done without, but it was part of the battle plan. The first session was scary, that's the best word to describe it. I checked into the hospital in the morning and had to wait until late afternoon for them to prepare my chemo. It came in the form of bags that looked very similar to a drip, with the addition of a large toxic label emblazoned on the bag itself. I liked to think that I was conscious of how I treated my body and cared about what went into it, so the toxic warning sign was rather distressing.

Why would I want to fill my body with something that would be harmful and toxic? I originally consoled myself with the thought that it was killing all of the bad cells, those renegades that were causing the trouble, but then I read that it was also killing off other good things in its path. I realised that it was not such a good thing for my body. I reasoned with myself and thought about the many other harmful things that I had probably unknowingly exposed myself to over the years, and decided to trust the oncologist. I was told that my reaction to the first session of chemo might be vomiting, and that that was a normal reaction and nothing to be overly concerned about.

It all sounded like such a horrible situation. What's more, if I was in pain when I laughed, how much worse would it be when I vomited?

As the nurses put the cannula in my hand, I could feel the fluid flowing through my veins as the line was flushed in order to ensure that there were no blockages and the chemo could flow freely. A little while later, the first of the two chemo bags were ready and they were attached to the cannula; they would be my buddies for two days. It was a strange sensation when the chemo entered my veins: it felt like ice-cold fluid flowing into my body. Then after a few hours the nausea began, a feeling of seasickness that I still remember now. Next, the bottom of my feet began to tingle, as well as my hands, and at that point I just wanted it all to end. The first couple of sessions were the worst, mostly because as I vomited the pain from the wound was excruciating. The wonderful thing was that by the time I got to my third or fourth session the vomiting stopped and I just had to deal with the nausea and other side effects that the chemo offered, such as the tingling of the hands, complete numbness of my feet and diarrhoea.

There were other side effects that I was not told about but read in the leaflets that were given to me. It seemed that different brands of chemo had slightly different side effects. Two out of the three brands of chemo that had been recommended for me mentioned infertility, whereas only one mentioned alopecia.

Under the heading 'Fertility' I read, 'Your ability to conceive or father a child may be affected by taking this drug. It is important to discuss fertility with your doctor before starting treatment.'

Another information leaflet for another drug stated: 'Your ability to conceive or father a child may be affected by taking this drug. It is important to discuss fertility with your doctor before starting treatment.'

The Campto brand of chemo stated that 'Alopecia was very common and reversible …Campto is indicated for the treatment of patients with advanced colorectal cancer, in combination with 5 fluorouracil and folinic acid in patients without prior chemotherapy for advanced disease.' So it was two-to-one with the fertility thing: I had not really considered having children before, but as the option was possibly being taken away from me I realised that I was in a bit of a serious situation.

My oncologist had advised that I have treatment every two weeks. That gave my body the time to recover from each session and I was grateful for the break, as I had not realised just how much the chemo would affect me. I was in hospital for two days each time the sessions took place, and by the time I finished the first session I was unable to walk or communicate much because of the combination of pain from the surgery and nausea from the chemo.

As each session was finished, Wayne would put me in a wheelchair and take me down to the car. The passenger seat would already be reclined, ready and waiting for me to fall asleep for the duration of the journey back to Sheffield. I would wake up to find myself in bed and then the pangs of nausea would ensue. I would use a stick to bang on the floor for assistance, we thought of using a bell, but Wayne objected to the idea that he was a dutiful Jeeves!

I took my anti-nausea tablets for three days once I returned home. Not much eating or drinking would take place during that time and I was bed-ridden. After the three days had passed I was a little more able to communicate, able to eat the basics, to walk around and to bathe. The routine was that I would have a total of about seven days of being out of it, which began with three days of nausea, then moved on to being listless for about two days; by about day five I was approachable but still needed physical rest, then by the seventh day I was rested and ready to enjoy the seven days of consciousness. If for whatever reason all didn't go according to the pattern, I was highly disappointed and became a little discouraged, but there were only a couple of occasions when I reacted adversely to the chemo and it left me unable to function. I counted my blessings. During week two when I had more energy I would read about nutrition and healing to help to strengthen my body. I managed all of the administration that went with having a critical illness and owning a property, and all of that kept me busy enough not to have to think too deeply about what could be, but to focus on the end result.

So the beat went on. Everything was going well and according to plan; I felt that I was winning the battle. Chemo continued for about four months and all seemed fine until a chest x-ray came back with a result I hadn't expected. It looked as though the little mites had been tricking me, making me believe that the battle was all mine.

The chest x-ray showed a shadow on my lungs. According to my oncologist it could have been just that, but he wanted to be safe not sorry. Upon his recommendation, my next session of chemo was to be an increased dose. I was devastated. Up until that point I had kept things together and was able to remain calm. I knew I was beating it, but the results from the chest x-ray were a major setback that took the legs from beneath me. I was tired, so tired of it all. I agreed to the recommendations of my oncologist; did I have a choice? I had fought hard to get to that point and if increasing the strength of the chemo made the difference between me living and dying, I chose to increase and live.

The new dose of chemo would be given during my next session two weeks later. I was told about the risks, which were the same as before, but the difference was, if I continued long term with the stronger dosage it was more likely to have adverse effects on organs such as my heart and liver and would be highly likely to affect my fertility in a negative way. That was something both my oncologist and I agreed we did not want, so the quicker we could annihilate these intruders the better.

The week leading up to that session was not the greatest, and I lost it for the first time. I broke down and said that I didn't want to do it anymore. I was tired, scared and just did not have the fight left in me. I remember sitting in my bedroom at Wayne's house, facing Elaine and a friend of mine and sobbing uncontrollably. They were both stunned for the first few minutes and did not know how to react and what to say, it was completely out of character for me to behave in that manner. After a few minutes, Elaine realised that something needed to be said and began to console me. The encouragement she gave me seemed to do the trick, as she explained that I had dealt with everything so well, and had been really positive up until that point. I was allowed to break down and cry and there was nothing wrong with that, it was a good thing. As she spoke I realised that I had taken the whole situation on and was dealing with it in my usual fashion – by myself. Even though everyone around me really wanted to do more for me I was so used to shouldering everything and just getting on with it because it was alien for me not to be in control of situations. Yet I definitely felt that I could not leave things to chance this time.

After that day, I realised that I needed a break. I could fight the battle but I needed to refresh myself physically, mentally and spiritually: I needed to be inspired.

My cousin Suzannie had visited from Canada during the summer and her descriptions and photos of the country grabbed my attention immediately. She said I was welcome to visit any time. I thought about it and then decided that no matter what, after my next chemo session, I was going to take a break for a while and just let my hair down a bit and get away from the serious stuff. I spoke to my oncologist and he agreed, saying that as long as my visit was no more than a month, I had the go ahead to travel and have some fun. I was delighted. My health cover was organised by my work place (who had been absolutely superb during the whole process) and it enabled me to have the same treatment in a private hospital anywhere in the world that I chose to visit.

I so needed to escape and to have something to look forward to, so I called my cousin Suzannie in Toronto. I would not normally have imposed, nor taken up an invitation to visit someone unless I knew them quite well, but my cousin seemed cool and she seemed to want to spend more time getting to know the family. I felt as though I had known her for years, even though I had only spent two weeks with her. I suppose that was how it was supposed to work with family.

I began my research into airfares, browsing online and trying to find the best airfare for July. I thought I ought to give myself the usual week to recover from chemo and then I would be fit to travel. I didn't plan to do much during the first few days of my stay there, as Suzannie would be at work until the weekend and my other cousins (who I hadn't met either) were at work too. A friend of mine had moved to Toronto from Huddersfield, so I also had the opportunity to catch up with him, too. I was excited and the planning took my mind off the dreaded chemo session! I didn't care how tough the next session was, just as long as I was ready to take the flight a week later. Canada was my dangling carrot and it helped to give me the incentive to hold it all together.

The day of the chemo session finally arrived and all went according to plan. I had the usual two days of chemo at the hospital, but the reaction to the chemo was slightly different. I had become accustomed to the tingling of the fingers and feet as the chemo made its way through the line into my veins, but this time the nausea pre-occupied me, along with the smell and taste of metal that kept my olfactory senses in overdrive.

Two days in hospital and seven days at home gave me the necessary time to recuperate and strengthen my body just enough to make the journey. I believed that I had earned it. It was a very exciting time for me, especially as I hadn't ever thought of Canada as a holiday destination.

When I got off the plane the first thing that hit me was the heat; Toronto was hot in July! My cousins had warned me that it would be hot, but I had not realised just how hot they meant. I arrived early in the evening and there was quite a lot of activity at the airport, but the people seemed so happy and helpful. The place had a good feel about it. Everywhere I had visited up until that point ended up being a place where I wanted to live – I always had a very emotional connection to places. Having cancer had made me a little more realistic, a little more mature to say the least, but I still had some way to go!

I spent three weeks in Toronto and had a fantastic time filled with meeting family members for the first time, seeing a friend that I had not seen for many years, enjoying the many festivals, such as the Greek festival and the carnival, going to water parks and gorgeous restaurants, but the most poignant part of the trip was a gift from my cousin Neil. I had never met Neil before, but had heard many wonderful stories about him and his sister Jackie, who had moved from Huddersfield to Canada when they were young. They were my first cousins, my Mum's brother's children, and when they emigrated they were missed by all of the family. I didn't know what to expect at all, but what I encountered surpassed my expectations and impacted my life in a way that was crucial to my healing. Neil and Jackie were both great hosts and Neil's gift to me was an appointment with a nutritionist.

Neil's introduction to the nutritionist put me on the path to having a healthy diet and making changes to my lifestyle. This was enlightening and gave me the jolt I needed to begin taking care of myself. I had never seen food as important before; I viewed it as a way to give my body enough energy to function. I used to eat breakfast and one additional meal per day and I didn't really pay much attention to the nutritional contents of my meals. I saw eating as something that took up time, and because I could function on small amounts of food, I didn't eat much.

The nutritionist did a live cell microscopy test, where she pricked my little finger with a small needle and put a tiny amount of blood onto a slide, which she then studied under a microscope. I was amazed that a minuscule amount of blood told me so much about the state of my body and what a state it was in!

Until that point I don't think I had ever really cared for myself. I hadn't really taken responsibility for my internal health or seen my body as something that needed to be cared for. I had just taken care of the superficial. I exercised, indulged in beauty treatments and pampering, but never deeply considered what was going on inside my body. I realised that God was obviously trying to get my attention and that if I didn't listen I may be in a spot of bother (as if I wasn't already!).

The nutritionist showed me a laminated card with pictures that, from a distance, looked like kidney beans, but a closer inspection revealed that the shapes were all slightly different. Some shapes were almost circular, and others looked as though chunks had been taken out of them, which made them look rather odd. The nutritionist explained that they were all cells. The shapes on the left-hand side of the card were examples of unhealthy cells and the shapes on the right-hand side were examples of healthy cells. There were also different degrees or stages of health illustrated on either side of the card. The nutritionist had already had a peep at my cells through the microscope, and now it was my turn to view and compare my cells to the ones that I had seen on the laminated cards.

I looked through the microscope and saw my cells moving around, they were active but very misshapen. My cells looked like the cells on the left-hand side of the card, which were the unhealthy cells, but they weren't the cells at the top of the unhealthy side, they were the cells at the very bottom of the card. It was devastating to see the state of my body under a microscope. The things that I had learned about cells in school and during my beauty therapy training came flooding back. I knew that if I was unhealthy at a cellular level, I wouldn't last for long. I needed to somehow generate healthy cells and restore the unhealthy cells in order to regenerate a healthy me.

My cells were deformed and dying before my eyes. It was quite overwhelming for me, as I had always seen myself as basically healthy! I look back now and see how deluded I was, and how the dominant view – 'To look good, and feel great meant I was healthy' – was all a big lie.

Everything that I had thought to be true and had built life on was beginning to fall apart. My life was built on such flimsy material that when under duress everything began to fall apart. The truth was that what was on the outside wasn't a true representation of what was taking place on

the inside. I had listened to how others had described me and modelled myself upon that. The words 'beautiful', 'cute', 'gorgeous' and 'athletic' were words that had fed my ego and helped to shape me. I realised that my damaged cells were a true reflection of how I truly was and how I truly felt ... misshapen. I knew that in order to re-shape and re-mould myself I needed to begin at the cellular level, working from the inside out.

The nutritionist told me that she had collated information from the test and by looking at my tongue, eyes and skin. She gave me a pack of information, including a menu for a detoxifying broth, wheat-free food options, a two-week no salt, no sugar diet plan, and a list of recommended herbal supplements. It was all new territory to me, especially the no sugar part; me not eating sugar was like asking a dog not to chew a bone!

Neil noticed that it was quite a lot for me to take in. Back at his house he had what seemed to be a whole library on health and nutrition. He kindly allowed me to browse his bookshelves, and also recommended particular books that

41

I could purchase to learn more on the subject. Since I still had about two weeks left in Toronto with not much planned, it seemed like the perfect way for me to fill my days.

I read countless books, listened to tapes about cancer, doctor's views on cancer and how to go about healing your body. I read about herbal remedies that could aid in healing cancer, and foods that could aid in the healing of the body. It was as though someone had directed me to go to Toronto to meet my family, who, in turn, would introduce me to the nutritionist in order to help me to learn more about how to heal my body and re-evaluate my lifestyle. I truly believe to this day that those encounters played a huge part in helping to save my life!

While in Toronto I lost my hair – it began to fall out after I visited the water park. I think it must have been the combination of the chemicals from the texturiser that I used to texturise my hair, the chemo (of course) and the chlorine from the pool. I had been dreading that moment, but because it was shedding slightly I hadn't noticed the patches that had begun to form. It was when I stayed over at my friend's and I woke up with clumps of hair all over the pillow that I was shocked.

Everyone in Toronto was so positive and had such a great sense of humour. It made a bad situation easier to deal with and I felt as though I was in the right place at the right time. My cousin bought me some headscarves to cover my patchy afro and I didn't put any lotions or potions on it for a few days. I thought that if I didn't tamper with it that it may not fall out and it might just grow back. But then it got to the point where I just couldn't stand it anymore, and feeling desperate to wash my hair because of the heat and sweat; that was when it happened. I lathered the shampoo and my hair began to fall at my feet like leaves in autumn. The hair follicles had become useless and could no longer hold the strands of hair in place. I got out of the shower and looked at my reflection in the mirror and I thought, "You look stupid, just get rid of it all." My baldhead could be hidden beneath the scarves, so it was just pride that had kept me from removing the patches of hair that remained. I had done well to keep my hair during the five months of chemo, but its loss was the straw that broke the camel's back for me. I decided that I didn't want to have any more chemo, I wanted to give it a break as my body was beginning to talk to me and the hair loss definitely wasn't speaking to me in a positive manner. I called my cousin into the bathroom as she had seen the patches that were forming before, and I needed her help.

"Suzannie, I need you to help me to take my hair off. It's pointless having these patches on my head, they look ridiculous."

I had never seen my cousin lost for words as she was a sharp cookie and nothing usually fazed her, but I could see that she was clearly stunned.

"I don't know how you can be so calm. If it were me, I'd probably be crying, I'd be like, 'My hair'," she eventually said.

I sat down in the bathroom and we got on with the task in hand. I looked at her and as she pulled gently at the hair at the back of my head, which came out with ease, I smiled and said, "Now I'm going to have new hair, brand new hair."

We both laughed as we pulled the clumps of hair from my head, my cousin with tears in her eyes at times, but it was a great bonding experience. We put my hair in a bag and I

looked at my new, bald reflection in the mirror. What a picture! Hair had always been such a statement in our family. We were always told that as women our hair was our beauty. I had become fed up with the cultural pressures about hair and I had cut my hair before I went to Egypt so it was short anyhow. I must have known deep down that I would lose my hair, because if I had been at the stage where hair mattered I probably would have been devastated by the loss. The main concern for me was not how I felt, but how others would see and treat me.

Nothing is a coincidence in this life and people come into our lives for reasons, seasons or a lifetime. Each one of my cousins taught me something while I spent time with them, and so many beneficial things happened in such a short period of time. It seemed as though I was on a crash course for life's lessons while I was there, but the one thing that struck me the most and has stayed with me was that they loved and cared for me so much. They didn't want anything in return, they didn't even know me but I was accepted into their homes, into their lives and into their hearts, and it seemed a normal and natural thing for them to do. I was so grateful.

The time had come to return to England, but I somehow felt stronger and better equipped to fight the battle. On my return I decided to sport the new look with the headscarves, as I had not quite built up the courage to show my bald head … plus it was colder in England.

CHAPTER FIVE

Navigating Unknown Territory

On my return to England I would sometimes forget that I didn't have hair, until Wayne would say, "Gosh, sis, it's scary, you really do look like me." I also had everyone else telling me that I was Wayne's 'mini-me', the running joke of the bald season.

I went to see my oncologist on my return and his staff took another x-ray that brought positive results, showing that the shadow on the lungs was no longer there. I was ecstatic and asked my oncologist whether it would be necessary to continue with the chemo. I was even happier when he said, "No. I think you have been through enough and you have been a good girl, go and have some fun and come back to me in a month so we can do some checks."

I was free, free from the chemo, free from hospital beds, free from the schedule of doctors' appointments, free from scans, free from x-rays and finally free from blood tests.

As time had gone by it had become increasingly more difficult for the nurses to find my veins, so in order for the bloods to be taken easily they inserted a cannula for the chemo. The line had been inserted through the main vein in my right arm, and enabled the chemo to be fed directly into my system. It was a brilliant idea, as it prevented me looking like a pincushion on every visit to the hospital and it also helped for the bloods to be taken in a jiffy. I liked the line, it dangled a bit a times and meant short sleeves couldn't be worn without quizzical stares and questioning, but now, with the oncologist's blessing, it was time for my dear companion to go.

The procedure for removal wasn't as nauseating as the procedure for insertion. I would never forget feeling sick to my stomach during the procedure when they inserted the line into my arm. My veins were so small and they didn't like being poked and prodded around, so they would run for cover at each attempt to extract that much-needed red fluid from them. I guessed that my veins were definitely a true reflection of my personality, cheeky yet introverted at times. I was sure that they were as happy as me that the painful but necessary process was over.

I left London Bridge hospital not really knowing what my next move would be, but knowing that it was time for me to spread my wings a little and to take a much earned break. Even though all I had done was exchange one bed for another over the months, it had been quite a gruelling, draining and tedious process. I had tried to make the best out of the situation, and welcomed the hospital and home visits from friends, colleagues and family members. It had been a rollercoaster ride, but I knew that I hadn't dealt with how I really felt about the whole ordeal, as my focus had been on the physical battle. I felt the time had come for me to begin the psychological processing. All of the doctors and geneticists couldn't really explain how and why I had contracted cancer. I had lost count of the number of times I had been asked, "Has anyone in your family ever had cancer? Who was it? What type of cancer was it? How long ago was that?"

The answers to most of the questions were no, and the only person who was relevant was my great Uncle Walter, who was truly great, but he had throat cancer not bowel cancer. It was a mystery to them and to me, but I knew that there had to be more to it than met the eye, and I couldn't leave it unresolved. I began searching for some answers, as I was certain that in getting some of the answers I would also find a way to clear the cancer that had invaded my life.

It had been agreed that I would return to work part time in the New Year and wanting to spend Christmas in a warm place, I spent a few months travelling around the Caribbean, between Jamaica, Antigua, Montserrat, Tortola and St Thomas. It was a very therapeutic time!

On my return to England I knew that I was truly back to reality, back to the flat in London, back to work, back to bills, back to the monotony that would probably drive me crazy, but it was necessary. I returned to London, thankful that I had had the opportunity to travel and see my friends and family members during my 'time out', and grateful that I was still alive and able to work. It was time to resume everyday life. I had conflicting emotions as part of me wanted to go back to normality and reality, but then another part of me just wanted to run away and live a simple life on an island in the Caribbean. The practical side of me took over and won the battle, it was time to get back to reality.

Returning to work was quite overwhelming, as the word had spread as to why I had been off. I had gone from being an extremely private and mysterious person to being what seemed like an open book. I had to get over that, but it was hard and that was when I was thankful that I was only working three days per week. Partners in the firm came up to the reception desk to ask me if I was okay, which I found a rather an uncomfortable situation to be in. I didn't want people feeling sorry for me. I had never been soft, weak or vulnerable in my life, but somehow this illness had brought about circumstances in my life that I had previously only watched play out from a distance in other people's lives. It had never crossed my mind that those things could ever happen to me – not that I thought that I was superhuman (then again, maybe I did and that was why it was such a shocking situation for me).

I could sense that people were treating me with kid gloves, and that they just didn't know what to say or do at times, but I had become accustomed to the discomfort of others in my presence. Either they were open and asked too much or they acted as though nothing had happened and got on with business as usual, but that was okay with me. I tried to help others as much as possible because I knew it was also uncomfortable for them, too, at times.

I was given basic duties to complete during the first few months back at work, and that gave me much time to think. It was then that the thought came back to me. "There had to be more to my illness than met the eye." I needed to explore a little. I began to write again. I would write my thoughts in my journal, and as I wrote the thoughts unravelled. I realised that life was not all that I had expected, and before I had become ill I was extremely unhappy. I had filled my life with things such as parties, restaurants, people, cleaning, sex, work, travelling, shopping and studying, but I still didn't feel satisfied or fulfilled. I began to explore why I had filled my life with all of these things and not found any real type of happiness. I wondered why I felt so empty and what could stop me feeling that way.

CHAPTER SIX

Facing The Real Enemy

As time went by at work I began to look around me and wonder why it was that God had allowed me to live. There were people with families, loved ones who had been in similar situations, and they had fought a good fight but never survived. I had returned to London to live alone; the job that I returned to had little or no prospects; I had stopped studying; I was not in a relationship and could not foresee one in the future, and it didn't make any sense that God had allowed me to live. I suppose I did ask him to spare my life, but was that the only reason that I was still alive? Had I gone through so much to continue in the same vein and not *do* something of significance with my life? The whole thought process began to depress me, and then I began to think that maybe God had got it wrong, that I shouldn't have been alive, because I was just taking up space and not serving any real purpose.

Free from cancer, with a future restored to me, it was at that point that my life began to take an accelerated downward spiral. I would put on a brave face at work, but when I got home in the afternoons I would cry, write, scream or just sit in an almost vegetated state, listening to music. During that time I was writing in my journal and there were a few things in particular that were really bothering me: the lack of relationship with my father and the abuse that I had suffered as a child. They were the two things that hurt me so much to speak about that I rarely let the feelings come to the surface.

During this time of exploration, it came to my attention that rather than deal with those things, I had buried them and pretended that they didn't exist, until one day my body began to tell me that there was something eating away at my insides that needed some attention. I would have continued to keep things wrapped up neatly if cancer had not caused the contents of my being to seep out and disrupt my neat and tidy life. When I began to face the truth and to know the psychological dimension to my illness, I couldn't cope. I didn't know how to get rid of the feelings of loneliness, hurt and anger; the line between work and my private life couldn't be drawn anymore because I couldn't get the thoughts out of my mind.

I was still seeing the Occupational Health therapist at the time, and I explained to him that I found it difficult to settle back into work; it had been overwhelming. He recommended that I go and see a psychiatrist to talk things through, as he believed I had been through a lot and it was normal to feel overwhelmed and to struggle with everyday life. I spoke to my manager at the time and she seemed a little surprised; the old Marcia would never have broken down – she was tough and just got on with everything. It was hard for me to admit, but I could feel myself going into meltdown.

The sessions with the psychiatrist were horrendous at first. The idea of speaking to a complete stranger, who I knew was evaluating my mental state, was not my ideal solution. I had always dealt with situations in my own way, and for some doctor to be questioning me in order to come up with a prognosis that I could be crazy, was not a situation I would normally have put myself in. I was wary of him, and he could tell. It was as though he was just waiting for me to go through the stages in order to be able to work with me.

One day, during one of my 50-minute sessions, I didn't feel like answering any questions or talking at all. I was told by the psychiatrist that if I wanted we could end the session early, or just sit in silence until the session was due to finish. That was the worst thing that he could have told me, as it just made me think that he didn't care at all, and was only there to collect his fee. I couldn't figure him out and because of that I found it very difficult to open up. But after about the fifth session, we began to get to the root of my problem.

It was about a month before my thirtieth birthday, and everything seemed to be coming to a head. I felt drained; I had spots all over my face; no matter how much I slept, I still felt tired; I wasn't really eating, and nothing at all excited me. I left work that day and headed to my session, but couldn't really speak; I just sat slumped in the leather bucket seat in the psychiatrist's office and went through the drill. I had filled in charts about my thoughts and thought processes. I handed them over to him, he read them carefully, and began to discuss them with me, but quickly realised that the session needed to take a different direction.

After a few questions I spoke about what was really on my mind. I told him about the sexual abuse that I had suffered as a child, and that of late I couldn't stop thinking about it and that it was affecting my every waking hour. He looked at me and after gaining more detail about the abuse he proceeded to tell me that I was an extremely strong character. I had carried the information around with me for approximately 20 years and got on with life as normal, but never dealt with it. At some point or the other it was bound to surface, and now it was time to deal with it in order for me to have a lasting relationship with someone and to be able to trust. It all fell into place for him, as we had spoken about all of my previous relationships up until the point of me beginning therapy. All of the relationships were ones that didn't require long-term commitment, for one reason or the other. I had purposely kept every man at a distance, physically or psychologically; subconsciously I wasn't ever going to allow anyone to get close enough to hurt me again. I was referred to a psychotherapist at The

Priory, and my psychiatrist advised that I continue my sessions with him, too.

The psychotherapist at The Priory seemed very nervous, not self-assured like my psychiatrist. It wasn't easy opening up to total strangers, as I was the type of person who was so used to carrying my own baggage, but I was tired of being tired. I saw my therapist once a week, and it took a good month for me to settle with her. The thing I learned in the short time that I had therapy was that I could be extremely honest and open about how I felt. Sometimes I went a little too far with my therapist and ended up feeling bad for the things that I said and the thoughts that I had. I was at the point where I didn't care what many people thought and would continue down the honest and open path in a militant manner.

My therapist and I settled after having an open and honest discussion about discrimination and prejudice, and what it felt like for me to be black in a predominantly white environment. It was an interesting discussion, and made me realise that she was a genuine and understanding person with a wonderful heart and I began to open up to her. The layers of the onion were being peeled.

Sometimes I would be able to take the stinging sensation and hold back the tears, but at other times it was as though the intensity of stripping back particular layers was too much to handle, and it opened up an endless floodgate. I hadn't cried about those areas of my life before, as it wasn't my policy to show emotion. I thought that it was a sign of weakness. We didn't really do the emotion thing in my family, but for the first time in as long as I could remember I cried, and it brought a real sense of relief for me.

With my thirtieth birthday approaching, the combination of two therapy sessions a week began to take its toll, and I began to feel increasingly burdened. Often by the time I got to my session I was physically and mentally exhausted. We spoke as usual about my thought charts, but I was tired. I was offered medication, which I refused to take. It was then that my psychiatrist encouraged me to think about being admitted to The Priory for two weeks. I was encouraged that this would allow me to concentrate on my therapy, as obviously the combination of therapy and my lifestyle weren't allowing me to make progress.

He said, "It will be great for you. Think of it as a health farm. It is lovely there and you will be taken care of instead of you taking care of everyone." I heard the word 'farm' and immediately translated it into 'funny farm'. I said to myself, "I'm not going to a funny farm." So I declined his offer, but he insisted that in order for me to rest and make specific time for myself, it would be the best way to move forward and get better. I told him that I had plans for my birthday and explained what they were. He responded by asking me if I would cancel them. I thought about it and wondered what reason I would give to everyone for cancelling? I didn't want people to know where I would be going, so what would I say?

The psychiatrist seemed to read my mind and then the suggestion was put forward that, rather than cancel my celebrations, maybe I could go into The Priory after the celebrations. At least I would be in a more relaxed state, and I wouldn't have to give explanations to everyone. That sounded like a good plan, as I didn't want to let my friends and family down. I wasn't that bothered about celebrating, but everyone else was, and they kept reminding me that it was a blessing that I was still alive.

There was a dinner organised with close friends and family, and a few of us had booked to stay in a hotel and visit the spa there. Everyone was more excited than me, but I went along with it, as that was partly my nature. I told my psychiatrist that I would think about the proposal and let him know within the next few days.

Life was one big struggle. To get up in the morning, to go to work and put on a brave face was a struggle. I didn't want to take medication to get me through the day; I had quite an addictive personality, and the idea of anti-depressants scared me; the thought of being hooked on a pill to get myself through the day, wasn't appealing. It seemed like the only way to sort the situation out, and quicken the process of getting my mind right, was to go to the 'funny farm'. I thought about what I wanted for my life, who I wanted in my life, and when I wanted those milestones to happen, and realised that if I didn't sort my life out I would never be able to have any of those things. It was time.

Skilled therapists had the ability to unlock the compartments of my mind, and help me to change the thought patterns that I had nurtured for so many years. I needed to change my thinking otherwise my life would never change. I was tired of the life I was living. I had to begin by removing the destructive thoughts from my mind, and I hoped it would end with me being able to let go of the past, and get on with living a life of peace in the present. I called my psychiatrist and asked him to book me into The Priory, and at the same time I confirmed that my stay would only be for two weeks. I prayed that I had made the right choice.

I don't recall what I did on the day before my admission to The Priory, my mind was quite hazy and it was hard to come to terms with the situation. The behaviour I displayed at that stage was that of discomfort and fear. If in an environment where I felt uncomfortable or threatened, I would just close down and become silent and contemplative. I supposed that if people looked closely they would have probably realised that I wasn't all there; I was too engrossed in the battle with my thoughts.

I recall on the Sunday– admission day – that I couldn't really summon up the energy to do much, I just lounged around and stayed in bed most of the day, knowing that I needed to check-in before six o'clock in the evening. I was having second thoughts but went into autopilot, and began to make my way to the tube station. I walked for a little while, and then my case seemed too heavy to carry, I felt drained. I had carried the same suitcase lots of times to catch many a flight, but this commute was different. The thought of carrying the suitcase when my final destination was The Priory just took away any energy that remained. I had spent the best part of two days in bed, but I didn't have the drive or enthusiasm to do anything. I returned to the flat and called a cab to take me to Bromley.

It was protocol for the admission of patients to be completed by a nurse and a doctor. The doctor on duty happened to have an aunt who was a doctor in Huddersfield, and he also thought he was a comedian. I really wasn't in the mood for his humour. He was quite cynical but I give him his due, he was persistent and continued professionally with the task in hand; to delve deeper into the mind of Marcia. I told him that I was not really in the mood to talk and he asked, "Is that a hint?"

I just looked at him as if to say, "Give me a break, mister, ask your questions and leave me alone."

The night was quite long and I ended up watching television for most of it; I just felt unable to do anything else. At about midnight I managed to get to sleep and slept between seven and eight hours.

The following day was my first official day at the 'health farm'. I was thrown in at the deep end with a group therapy session, which turned out to be very beneficial and a nice bonding experience. I found myself going from one session to the next, and before I knew it, it was dinner time. I realised by the end of the day that I was at a crossroads in my life and I needed to decide which direction I wanted to take. The help I was given to put my past behind me and make way for the present was a blessing within itself. I was truly blessed and that was what I needed to begin to realise. At that stage I believed it about 60 per cent and was beginning to believe that I would get there in the end.

I was glad that I had acknowledged the issues in my life, and due to my new found awareness I could move on to understand and accept them. I was also aware that the decisions I would have to make would be difficult. I realised the only reason I did the job I did was to pay my bills as I didn't get any real fulfilment from it. The girls were lovely, that was the beautiful thing, but the girls weren't responsible for my mental stability and well-being. I realised that the only person who was responsible for me was myself and that was difficult and daunting to accept. The thought of making the right choices and decisions seemed overwhelming, but what were the right choices and decisions anyway? Only time would tell.

My mothering, care-taking characteristics were not ideal for bringing balance into my life. I was always mothering or taking care of someone because that was what I had always done. The underlying confusion had raised its ugly head with critical illness being the catalyst for contemplation. The metamorphosis had begun; it would take time to be completed, but the wheels were in motion. I looked forward to being able to breathe again without thinking, "Why am I breathing like that and what does it mean?" The saying that a leopard can't change its spots sprang to mind, but I wanted to have faith in myself and know that it was possible to change my thoughts, which in turn would change my life.

The plan was to rid the compartments of my mind of the many skeletons that were neatly stored away so that new things could come my way without a collision occurring. Life was to be lived and enjoyed. To accept myself and other people, to forgive them and to know myself were the challenges that I had battled with and were key to the direction my life would take. I had many questions:

"If I resumed my studies, what would I do with my qualification once I had completed it?" "Should I begin to try and have children?" "Should I wait and do things in the order deemed correct by certain parts of society (marriage and then children)?"

The one thing that became more evident was that I needed to deal with my past before I could move onto the future.

I generally struggled with socialising at The Priory. On warm days the garden was often filled with people, many of them smoking, but the good thing was that there were smiles on the faces of the individuals as they spoke about their illnesses. I found it strange that depression was classified as an illness and not a state of mind.

The professionals told me that it was an illness because the brain wasn't functioning to the best of its ability due to a chemical imbalance; hence there was a need to re-balance the whole. I withdrew and spent the rest of the evening in my room, as I felt I'd reached the limit of my small talk that day.

My bouts of paranoia magnified while I was at The Priory; maybe that was why I was there. I also thought that I had been admitted for self-healing, not to provide an emotional crutch. That thought made me want to go home. It was a consolation that the staff no longer treated me as a possible suicide case and it made me feel liberated in a strange way. I began to feel down, I definitely didn't feel like smiling – the idea of sitting in the garden with the smokers wasn't enticing. As usual I had set myself up for a fall with my puritanical manner. "No, I don't drink coffee or alcohol, nor smoke cigarettes, I just don't like doing that." Perhaps, to other people, I seemed like a puritan or a perfectionist, but on the other hand they probably didn't give a toss about me! Nevertheless, it was lovely to talk to the patients, as they were the ones that I learned a lot from.

The issue wasn't that I didn't want to live or that I didn't value my life, it was that I needed to appreciate my life and get rid of the things that caused contention.

I returned from my next therapy session rather frazzled; it had been tough to speak in detail about the abuse I was subjected to. I had to describe the details of the abuse from the first time it happened and where and why I thought it happened. It was tough, and before I knew it I was in tears and sobbing like a baby. I regained my composure after a while and then continued to talk about the whole experience. Most distressing was the fact that at the time I felt as though I had done something wrong and had been carrying it around like a ball and chain for all of those years. In my mind I was the one who had made the indecent act occur and I felt dirty and guilty about the whole thing. When my uncle decided he was finished with me I was lying there feeling numb and that was when I discovered the bleeding. He told me that it was okay, so I went from the box room to the bathroom across the hall and cleaned myself up. The one thing that upset me when I look back was the fact that the house wasn't empty. I recall Mum was there, where in the house exactly I don't remember, but she was there. I blamed her in a way for not noticing. That was why the whole drinking thing upset me because I knew, or I hoped, that her being sober would have stopped him in his tracks.

I went to pick up some lunch and was about to sit down but then saw a large crowd of other patients and it just put me off. I really didn't feel like interacting or being sociable. It wasn't that the others were getting on my nerves, I just felt I needed the time to organise a few things in my head. I had another session with my therapist the following day at four o'clock, and then I was due to see my psychiatrist towards the end of the week for a quick chat. The nice thing, actually it was a beautiful thing to see, was that my psychiatrist had a real sense of purpose. He had been blessed with skills and ability which he used daily to affect people's lives.

During my sessions, my therapist pointed out that my abuse was not a secret anymore; she also asked if I had cried after the abuse had taken place? I didn't recall crying after the abuse had occurred. Maybe, she asked, that was why the thought of crying was a bad thing to me, as I associated it with the abuse.

I also realised that subconsciously I didn't choose to go out with or have sexual relationships with men who were of a big build. Instead I would choose psychologically overpowering men. Domination was something that my first sexual experience entailed and subconsciously ever since then, that was the way my mind perceived that sexual experiences should be. Sex wasn't a pleasurable experience for me it was more like a chore. That made me think that I shouldn't have any sexual contact with anyone or make any commitments of any type until I was psychologically healed. I felt dirty and used most of the time after having sex, and I hated those feelings.

Most of my sexual relationships had followed the same pattern. My subconscious had been choosing what it thought to be right, but in my conscious state I didn't want that anymore. There was work to be done to treat myself better and respect my body and soul. If I couldn't do that for myself no one else was going to come into my life and do it for me. I would be single, childless and lost for the rest of my life if I didn't decide to make different decisions. That wasn't the picture I wanted to paint for my future.

The picture I saw was that life wouldn't be all rosy – there would be ups and downs – but I saw myself with a loving husband and children, living in a place that was warm for most of the year. The education of my children would be paramount, probably because those avenues weren't available to me, and I believed that it would give them a sound knowledge of themselves and the world they would be living in.

I went to my session the following morning and began to talk about my relationships and how they had been affected by my abuse. I felt that the abuse had made me very cautious about whom I chose to be with, in terms of physical size, as I didn't want to be dominated or overpowered. The thing that surfaced during my session was that I had chosen guys who had repeated that abuse in different ways, such as infidelity. Because I didn't have a good self-image, I chose relationships that mirrored that. What I also realised was that I often chose guys who would stand out in a crowd, because they were supposedly the guys who my family would approve of in the long run. The men in my family seemed very capable, in many ways they were multi-talented.

I had bought into their idea of what was suitable for me, of what they thought I deserved. The projection of this false image meant that I would try to attract the popular guy. The image I projected was sparkly, as I believed that in order to be liked I needed to act in a particular way, and be all *they* wanted me to be in order to remain attractive to them.

I put up with men and their infidelities because that was what I thought I deserved, and the abuse made me continue to tolerate their behaviour. I wondered whether I would put up with the same nonsense in my next relationship? It was early days, and I needed to write and review the information I was collecting about myself at a later date. I wasn't comfortable with my self-image and the personal traits that I possessed, and the sessions made me see that I had a lot of work to do.

It was my time to learn, heal and make some decisions. I had a vision that one day I would be able to sit on the balcony of a white, wooden, beach-fronted house, watching the lovely sunset and I would just take a deep breath, inhaling the aromas of my surroundings, but also remembering what I had been through to get to that stage of my life. The exhalation would be a release of all of the emotions and memories from the past, which would make way for the future that, once upon a time, was only a dream. It would be a wonderful reality, and that would be the day I would work towards.

The manifestation of that vision would be my driving force; the path would be bumpy at times, but would be worth it. What I almost didn't write, was that I saw a wonderful somebody walking up behind me and slowly putting his arms around my shoulders; then he pressed his nose into my neck, then he continued moving his nose from one side of my neck to the other. His presence would be a special presence and that alone would be worth the sacrifice made along the way. The love of the faceless, attentive companion was appealing and realistic, and the icing on the cake would be a little Marcia or two! I would embrace it when the time came; it was always such a relief to the soul to be truthful.

Another day on the farm I decided to attend the Coping with Anxiety workshop. The counsellor there explained about core behaviour and how the core of a person needed to be penetrated in order for them to change the behaviour patterns that had been formed. It made sense, and I realised that a behaviour pattern began its formation for me the day that my Mum and Dad split up (thought pattern: belief that men found it difficult to be monogamous), continued when my Dad said goodbye to me, and gave me what I remember as my last proper, loving hug as a child (thought pattern: the feeling of abandonment), and the final thing was when I was sexually abused (thought pattern: feelings that in my relationships all men saw me as a sexual object, and that sex was the main focal point in any relationship that I had).

These revelations were major breakthroughs. I continued working on my past, walking towards the present, hoping to embrace my future.

I felt as though I had deviated from the path slightly with regards to my spirituality – there had been so many distractions – but the one thing I continued to do was to pray daily; God had been good to me and I was truly grateful. It had got to the point where I had had to be admitted to a psychiatric hospital in order for me to be able to say that as well as suffering from everything else, I was suffering from depression, or suppression, or whatever anyone wanted to call it. I had suppressed feelings of happiness or love and had done so for years, just in case the other person got scared and ran away from me. I suppressed my feelings and protected myself because I was scared that I might give too much, and that others could hurt me and take advantage of my feelings. I thought I was protecting myself from any harm that could come my way, but because of the suppression, I hid myself away so much that I had a problem with my true identity. It wasn't a matter of finding the old Marcia; it was a matter of creating a new Marcia so that I could cope in the world.

I remembered times when I felt that to hug or to kiss someone I had to suppress my feelings and internalise my emotions. As a result of that, my happiness would turn into sadness, and then into depression. I would then blame myself for behaving in a manner that made the other person run away, but after analysis I saw that I hadn't done anything wrong; I had just been listening to myself and doing what came naturally to me. I worried too much about what the other person would think or feel, and what the implications would be with regards to me. I could see it all very clearly. Since the age of about 10 years old I had been a classic case of suppression, and I changed because change was forced upon me.

People around me couldn't cope with my behaviour, and instead of asking me, "What's up?" they told me that I was miserable and moody and that I needed to change. Rather than looking at the cause, they looked at the effect. Even though I knew the cause of my behaviour, I focused on the effects and tried to remedy them and the thing was, I knew that the effects were symptoms of my dis-ease with myself. What I needed to do was to continue to use medicine to cure the dis-ease. Just as I nourished myself with food, I needed to nourish my mind with things that could lead to peace and happiness.

In the Putting Therapy into Practice group session the counsellor asked, "Marcia, what do you want?"

I responded, "To be at peace with myself and to love and be loved in return."

The counsellor also asked me, "When you suppress your feelings, where do you put them? Where do you feel it the most?"

I had realised that I felt knots in my stomach. Moving to London at 17 years of age had put pressure on me to be tough, strong and to put on armour to protect myself. The armour was very difficult to remove, and I had to recognise when it was safe to do so and when it was not. I hoped that with time I would master that.

My life at that moment felt like I was driving a car. I was so busy observing the other drivers on the road, and trying to anticipate their every move that I was hindered from doing what I needed to do and remain focused. I was heading for a near-fatal accident, because I was paying too much attention to the other vehicles on the road, rather than focusing on mine.

I ran through the ideas for what I wanted to cover with my therapist in our session. I was thankful that she was such an amazing person and had brought me to the point where I felt I was making real progress. It was phenomenal how the mind worked when it was set to accomplish something. My therapist mentioned how impressed she was with my progress and that it could take people months to get from the point where I was, to the point to which I had arrived. I responded truthfully that it had taken me over 20 years to speak out, so it took me a long time to even begin to deal with the issue. I looked at it as all being relative; maybe other people didn't carry their problem around for as long as I did. It was swings and roundabouts.

In one of my sessions my therapist mentioned that my journals could be made into a book, I said, "We'll see". I enjoyed writing, and that was the most important thing to me. We had also discussed in previous sessions the issue of me confronting my abuser. I decided not to rake up the past, for the sake of my Mum more than anything else. If the time came to confront my abuser then I would, but I wasn't in the mood for confrontation. It was now all out in the open, and I couldn't imagine myself being the way I was before. I wasn't alone with the whole thing and it wasn't a deep, dark secret anymore; it was no longer a burden. I didn't felt guilty, dirty or fearful and I felt I had the tools to handle the situation if it were to rear its ugly head. I knew I would have to face him one day, but in the meantime I wanted to focus on getting my life in order. I left my session with a picture of what I wanted to do eventually; I saw a picture of me sitting outside my house near the sea with a laptop. To spend my days writing would be my ideal way to live, and I couldn't wait for that day to come.

After countless conversations at The Priory, I realised that people saw me as a cool, calm, quiet individual and that was fine. That was the core of who I was and how I remember being until I moved to London, but then I changed to become someone I no longer recognised. After removing some of the layers I realised that I was a reserved individual, who liked to observe situations before saying anything. I was no longer painfully shy, as with experience and maturity I had become quietly confident. It was definitely a nice place to be as long as I reminded myself that if or when things began to run away with me, that it was okay to be vulnerable and express emotions. I had felt the need to be perfect, but I realised that I no longer needed to aim to be perfect, because that was unrealistic.

To cherish each moment and be able to smile at life was a great achievement. It was a wonderful thing to be quiet and still because I felt like it, not because I thought that it was best for the audience. I explained it to another patient like this:

"Before, I felt as though I was in a dark room feeling my way around, not knowing which direction I needed to take to switch the light on, I was so afraid of the dark and of trying to find the light switch. Now, I am in the dark room and not so afraid of being there and feeling my way around. Knowing that when I am ready to switch the light on, I will go ahead and do so because I know where the light switch is. I feel more in control of my life. I feel more capable of being, and dealing with the Marcia who was anxious about being cooped up in the dark, scary place."

In my thirtieth year, I realised that I had always been that little bit different. My difference in opinions, style, colour, spiritual beliefs, partners and mind, all made up the person that I was. It had been a long and arduous journey, one with many obstacles and detours, but I felt that I was somehow on the right path now. It brought tears to my eyes and stirred up my soul. I felt as though I was getting closer to that person who was eight years old and as cheeky and opinionated as they came. That little forward-thinking girl had many plans for her escape to a better life, she was going to make a difference in the world. She was a unique girl, and had grown into a capable woman, but that little girl was still a big part of her. That little girl had enabled her to survive for such a long time in the world that seemed so full of dishonesty and pain. I thanked little Marcia for her existence and for bringing me to the next stage of my life where I felt I was about to blow the lid off things. It was time to say farewell to little Marcia.

Labels are put on many things in life for the sake of identification, so that people won't get confused, I suppose. I was beginning to know who I was and what I was capable of, so I no longer needed to label myself. It was important that I continued to be truthful and believe in my abilities. Life was becoming more beautiful, and as I meditated upon what had happened up to that point, I began to thank God for answering my prayer. In my heart I hoped that what I was experiencing would remain.

I had freedom from the thoughts that had once caused me pain, depression and anxiety. They returned fleetingly at times but I was no longer afraid, no longer fearful of the dark, lingering effects that clouded my vision and took me to a place where I had felt suicidal and lost. The separation of my parents at the age of five; sexual abuse by my uncle at nine; the alcohol addiction of my Mum from the age of eight; my departure from mum's home aged 11; being abandoned by my Dad; then living with my brother between the ages of 12 and 16 were all extremely influential experiences that helped me to form negative opinions of myself and others from a very young age. The opinion I had of myself wasn't the best, and those opinions consisted of guilt for appearing attractive, but believing that if men were attracted to me it was only because they wanted one thing. I believed that once they found out how dirty I was then they would leave. I believed that men weren't to be trusted as they all were cheats and liars. I believed that it was crude and rude to show anger, as only drunken, uncontrolled people did that.

I had so many beliefs, such as:

- I didn't want to appear attractive, as this was probably the reason why I was abused.
- I wasn't anything special.
- All men are cheats and liars, and the gift of flowers could be a sign of their guilt.

- Marriage was very risky and was no guarantee of fidelity.
- If I drank alcohol then I might become addicted.
- I should be seen and not heard.
- Men were the stronger sex.
- I should give the following to my partner in order to make him happy: sex whenever he wanted it (or he might leave/go elsewhere), meals, finance, love, advice, support, laughter, organisation, guidance, intellectual conversation, domesticity.
- I needed to be the best at all I did, otherwise don't bother.
- I shouldn't work just for money, but I should do something I loved and was passionate about.

I should try to help people the best way I could.

CHAPTER SEVEN

New Beginnings

I had found my way along the dark road to a section with light and it felt like such a relief. When I found myself wondering about tomorrow I would stop and take a deep breath; the action was no longer a sign of distress, but represented the day, the hour and the moment. The breath represented my struggles and victories, and my gratitude for those experiences that had made me become who I was on that day. I told myself that the present mattered, but it wasn't all that mattered.

I knew that I needed to work on the views I had of myself. I needed to be clear about what I wanted from life and who I wanted to be, and then I could work out how to get there. I realised that God had helped me so far and thought that maybe, He could help me with the rest of my journey. I was pleased that I was comfortable with the incredible metamorphosis that was taking place.

I began to realise that God was great and everything that happened in my life was for a reason; it all became apparent, given time. I was so grateful for all of my life experiences, and looked forward to many more, whether they were good or bad. I had many reasons to be alive, but I just needed to be still for a while in order to see so the way could become clearer. I felt as though I was about to burst. It was such a fantastic feeling that I wanted to hold onto, as it had been so long that I was brimming with excitement. I had gained so much in such a short time, and I had forgotten what it was like to feel so excited about life, about my life. I thanked God for all that He was and all that He had done to enable me to see. The path that I felt was once closed was open again and everything that I believed was possible could be. I was nurturing and giving time, love and attention to myself and I sensed that it was going to be just fine. I was fine, right there in that moment. I was being loving and kind towards myself, and enjoying doing so. The one thing that I needed to remember was that if I took the time out to process my thoughts, then that would in turn be useful to me and to others. Everything was being unpacked, and I thanked God for his guidance, love and clarity regarding my purpose.

I spent the days that followed going to sessions with my psychotherapist and talking about previous relationships, how I felt about the abuse, about my work and about the colour issue. I realised that my therapist had wanted to talk about the colour issue for a while, as we had exhausted the other subjects really. It was strange talking to a white person about how I had felt racism had affected me as a black person. I didn't really know how to express myself without causing offence, but at the same time it was my session and I needed to get things off my chest to be free from them to move on.

I was encouraged by my therapist to share my experiences of racism and prejudices. It wasn't until I began to speak that I realised how much hurt had been stored away. The experiences from childhood all the way to adulthood had made a firm imprint upon my character and the decisions that I had made. I was used to being in surroundings where the predominant set of people would be white and middle to upper class, and at times I sensed certain people would silently question my presence in particular settings because of my ethnicity. All of those experiences had left open wounds, but one of the ways for them to heal was to know my worth and my purpose. It was more likely that I would achieve the purpose for which I was born armed with that knowledge and understanding.

The conversation I had with my therapist made me see that there could also be reverse racism, and prejudices could stem from the insecurities of others. Life was too short to waste time with people who had such insecurities. All I could do was hope that a day would come when people would see past colour and look to the heart. If we could just live right with one-another, then we could see lasting change. I shared with her that I thought that our children needed to be aware of their history, not to breed anger and hatred, but to bring about an understanding of themselves and their position in the world. We needed to get past one person or set of people thinking that they were better than the rest for some superficial, nonsensical reason, and look to the heart of the matter. I began to see even more as I thought about racism and prejudice; it could also boil down to ignorance and fear, fear of the unknown, and fear of losing something to the unknown. Normally when fears were faced they were never as bad in reality as they were in the mind, and it was liberating.

Over time, the hurts that were stored up because of racist comments, the degrading looks and the invisible discrimination reminded me that in the midst of the hurts I had learned much. I was no longer naïve and I didn't need to be angry, unforgiving and bitter; that wouldn't make me any better than the ones who had mistreated me. I knew that wasn't why I was created, more importantly, I was on earth to do my part, to rise above adversity, ignorance, fear and make a way where the chances seemed few and far between. I remembered where my Mum and Dad had begun their journey, what they had done to make a way for their children … for me. I knew from the different stories they had shared that there had been many sacrifices made for our progression. I could also have been racist. I am sure I had been at some stage or the other, but it was about understanding other cultures and not being derogatory towards them.

The weeks in The Priory had helped me to reflect and to evict some of the demons that had taken up residence in my life. Things had happened to me, and I had kept them to myself for so long that they seemed like Goliaths in my life – too big to face. The mind was a dangerous place if left to its own devices; the junk was being removed and replaced with more nurturing thoughts. Life was beautiful. I could say that and really mean it as I could feel things that I had not felt in a long time, and they felt wonderful. I would no longer deny my true self, but would continue to be true to myself and with those around me.

CHAPTER EIGHT

Time To Be Free

I had travelled to different places always hoping that I would 'find myself'. I longed for a sense of belonging, and I hoped that my trip to Egypt in October 2000 would have been the moment where everything fell into place. It did, but not in the way that I expected.

I returned from Egypt with food poisoning and that illness revealed all that was going on with me physically and mentally, but I still had lots of questions about my spirituality.

I had spent almost 15 years running away from my surroundings trying to find myself, but then realised that wherever I went I still took all of my problems with me. Changing my surroundings couldn't change my mind and the thoughts that filled it; I had to do something that could help to change my mindset. I began to read the Bible more, but didn't really get it. I didn't know which faith to choose, but I had a slight belief that there was a God. I had begun to realise that I had been seeking something from about the age of 18 years old. I knew that there must be more, that I was meant to be more and accomplish more than I had up to that point, but I just didn't know what it was and where to find it. I thought that if I was successful in terms of monetary success then I would be complete. So, I sought success through reading books and listening to self-help material. I read about success – *The Magic of Thinking Big*, *The One Minute Manager* – books by Zig Ziggler and Og Mandino. I read and read and read, because I thought reading would give me knowledge and knowledge would give me power. I thought that I would have success with the combination of the knowledge that I accumulated, and the drive and determination I had. Once I was rich I would be free to do what I wanted and all would be great because money made the world go round.

I sought success, and along the way I met people who would speak to me about spirituality, about God and their view of God. I would speak to Buddhists, people into New Ageism, Muslims and Christians, and to me they all seemed to be seeking the same thing, peace and love. Some wanted to be loved, some wanted to know how to love, some wanted a combination of both and most seemed to want peace. At the heart of my beliefs was the view that all religions led to conflict, but I wished these people of faith well all the same. I believed that there was a God and that he created nature and us. It was all so complex that a higher power had to be involved, but that was where it all ended for me and I didn't ask any more on the subject.

Some of the men in my life had spoken to me about their God and frequently mentioned their spiritual beliefs (even if they didn't follow them to the letter). My boyfriends had often asked me what my beliefs were. They never got much out of me for I had been taught over the years that I wasn't to mention politics or religion in polite company, otherwise it may cause offence, so I made a conscious decision not to discuss either subject. I had my own views, my own beliefs, and I had come to my own conclusion about religion and politics. Politics was linked to religion and it saddened me that man had put God in a box and begun to use religion for his gain and personal agendas. I realised that the two subjects brought passion to a dull conversation, and could also bring about anger, which could in turn lead to conflict. I had so many unanswered questions, and it seemed that in order to get the answers I would need to delve deeper.

When I moved back to London in 2002 after recuperating in Sheffield with Wayne and Elaine, I wasn't sure which religion to choose, so I began with what I knew from childhood, which was the Bible. I started to do Bible studies via distance learning, and I gained more head knowledge about Christianity. My study programme was a simple study that took me through the books of Matthew, Mark, Luke and John. It was useful information but that's all I saw it as, information. I continued to read the Bible and prayed the best I could, just talking to God about things that would happen during my day. I would also ask lots of questions, which seemed pointless, as I didn't even really know whether I was being heard.

I would find myself waking up during the early hours of the morning and talking to God, then after speaking to Him I would find myself reading the Bible. I read the book of Revelation and was left really confused! I couldn't understand why it seemed like a foreign language to me and became frustrated that I couldn't work it out. I had always been able to find the answers to things, and this was no different (I thought), so there must have been a simple explanation that would be able to help me to interpret the Bible. But as time went on I had more questions than answers. I didn't really want to go to a church, even though I had promised God when I was ill that I would. Church just seemed too restrictive, the people seemed too perfect and I was far from that. I kept reasoning with myself that church really wasn't for me.

I had kept in touch with my cousin Nickelas over the years. We were the same age, but his life and upbringing were quite the opposite of mine. He was raised in a good, Christian home with Christian values, whereas I wasn't. We were like chalk and cheese, really, but we kept in touch over the years because he was such a lovely person.

One day while at work I received a call from him to say that he was getting married. I hadn't spoken to him for a while so it was quite a surprise, as I had never known him to even have a girlfriend! He gave me a potted history of his relationship and I was so happy for him.

I attended the wedding a few months later, which was a lovely affair. It was great to be able to spend time with family members that I hadn't seen for many years, and others that I had never met. I also saw another side to my Christian family members – they actually seemed quite fun and very happy! Towards the end of the evening, there were a few family members left at the wedding reception and I began to speak to Nickelas's sister, my cousin Karen. It was lovely to speak to her, as I hadn't seen her for many years. She always seemed so intelligent and well groomed

At the end of the evening, I was saying my goodbyes and getting ready to leave when she said,

"It was lovely seeing you, Mars, don't be a stranger now. Actually before you go, we have a guest minister visiting our church from Ghana at the moment. He's been here for a week already, but tomorrow will be the last Sunday he'll be ministering at our church."

Karen mentioned something about him being a prophet and explained what that was to me. All I heard and understood was that personal messages from God for particular individuals had been delivered through this man. I found it intriguing ... how could a man hear God speak like that?

As I mulled this over, the next question I heard from Karen was, "I know it's late now and you may be tired in the morning, but would you like to try and come?"

Before I knew it I was taking note of the address and time of the church service. I didn't have any plans for the following day and I could get the bus straight to Greenwich, as it wasn't far away from my flat. I could pop into the market afterwards too, so why not? I told Karen that I would see her the following day, and said goodbye to the rest of the family. I hoped that the visit to the church the following day would provide me with the answers I had been looking for.

I woke up early the following day as usual. Most days I was awake by 5.30 am, so would say a quick prayer and read the Bible. I had got into the habit of doing that for some reason, but didn't understand how or why. I did my usual stretches for about 20 minutes and then went for a run. I didn't run for long as I knew that I had to be back to get ready so that I would be on time for church. By the time I completed my morning routine, showered, ate breakfast, styled my hair and got dressed it was nearly 10 o'clock. I didn't want to miss the bus as Karen mentioned that the church service began at 11 o'clock, so began to organise myself and put essentials in my handbag. I could feel my stomach churning and I really disliked the feeling of anxiety. I slowed down, began my breathing exercises and kept going until I could feel my heart beat slowing down. I gave myself a minute and then I was good to go.

The journey to Greenwich didn't take long, but you could never tell with the number 47. Sometimes it was on time, then on other occasions you could be waiting for ages and then two or three buses would all come at once. I definitely didn't want to get there late, as I had no idea where I was going and didn't want to arrive all panicked and perspiring! Karen said their church met where the Greenwich Dance Agency was. I wasn't really familiar with the location, but followed the mini London A to Z that I carried with me at all times until I found the name of the road she'd given me. Upon turning the corner onto Royal Hill I spotted the Greenwich Dance Agency, it was quite a big building. I could feel my anxiety rising a little, as I realised that there must be a very large congregation at this church. I focused on my breathing again as I approached.

Karen had mentioned that I ought to ask for her upon arrival and someone would escort me to her. Sure enough, they seemed to know her really well and they took me to where she was sitting and she had saved me a seat.

I don't ever remember being in a place with so many people and calling it 'church'. I couldn't tell how many people were there, but there were definitely a few hundred and all I can remember thinking, over and over, was that there were a lot of people. I had no idea what to expect, but sat there just taking it all in. My cousin Karen introduced me to a young man called Jean-Marc; she told me he was a friend of my cousin Nickelas. Nickelas and his wife Melanie were on honeymoon in Jamaica, so Jean-Marc was sitting with Karen.

Dead on 11 o'clock the music began. I looked up on the stage and there was a full band, lead singer, backing singers, drums, keyboard and guitars, and they were going for it! People were singing along to the words that were projected onto two screens at the front of the hall on either side of the stage. I had no idea how long the music would last, but it was like a concert. It was loud, the people who were once seated were now standing up and singing, dancing and clapping to the music. I had never seen or experienced this before. It seemed strange, not at all as I expected church to be. I thought it rude not to join in, so I began to sing the words that were on the projector after listening to the songs a few times. I had always loved music, and when I was younger I had used to spend hours memorising lyrics from different artists like Anita Baker, Kashan, Luther Vandross and other Soul singers. The exposure seemed to have helped, because there was one song after the other, after the other, and I was trying to sing the lyrics along to the tune. Towards the end I got used to it as the songs seemed quite repetitive and the lyrics were simple to memorise.

I would always say to friends when we were out in clubs or bars that they should listen to the lyrics of a song carefully. I found that it was easy to get caught up with a wicked beat and not realise that the lyrics were completely degrading. Yet the lyrics of these songs seemed so pure, so innocent and so clean.

I looked around at the people, and they were singing the songs with all of their heart. Some were crying, some had their hands in the air, and there were two men at the front of the church really going for it and doing what I could only describe as skanking. They seemed quite young and I couldn't believe that people could be having such a good time singing songs like that. It made no sense.

The dancing and singing ended and then a man stood at the front of the church behind a lectern and greeted the people. Most responded and then he went on to introduce the minister from Ghana. The minister from Ghana stood up and walked to the front of the church. He was a very thin man, not so tall and I remember he had a big, brilliant white smile. He began to speak and I realised I was going to have to concentrate hard as it was quite difficult to understand him because of his accent. I listened intently. He spoke for a little while and then I saw him calling people to the front saying, "Can I pray for you?"

The way that he asked was so gentle and he was still smiling so brilliantly. He seemed happy as he spoke, excited, almost like a little child. I was amazed. He was saying things like the colour and door numbers of people, their first names, their last names, names of people within their family, and then he would choose from the people who were seated and begin to say things to them that seemed to be a secret or private. He would say things like;

"You've been asking God for a baby." The person would burst out crying, because it would seem that was the truth. Then he would say, "Thus sayeth the Lord, I have heard your prayers and I will give you not one but two children." Then he would go on to speak to the person about what the children would do when they were grown.

He spoke to many people like that, so many. It seemed so easy for him and the people seemed to listen very carefully to what he was saying, and some would respond by crying or falling on the floor. It all seemed very dramatic. Before I knew it the service had come to an end, the people applauded and thanked the man, he sat down and they started passing the offering basket around. I didn't quite understand what the purpose of the offering basket was, but gave what I had, which was a few coins.

I spoke to Karen briefly afterwards and she asked if I would come again, explaining that the following Sunday would be slightly different as the resident pastor would be back. I said yes, as I still hadn't got any real answers to my questions about the Christian faith.

The following Sunday came around very quickly and I found myself very excited about going to church. The people there had been very friendly, but I sensed there was more as to why I was feeling drawn to the place.

Upon entering the building the people were friendly as usual but I wanted to sit by myself, so as not to be influenced in any way. I sat towards the front of the hall and waited for the service to begin. The music started and I began to sing the songs, some of them were the same as the previous week and some of them were different. I sang the songs and as time went by the only way I can describe it is that my heart began to soften. There was a song with the lyrics;

Jesus, lover of my soul

Jesus, I will never let you go

You've taken me, from the miry clay

You've set my feet upon the rock

And now I know

I love you

I need you

And though my world may fall

I'll never let you go

My Saviour

My closest friend

I will worship you until the very end

Then there was another song;

When I think about the Lord

How he saved me

How he raised me

How he filled me

With the Holy Ghost

How he healed me

To the utter most

When I think about the Lord

How He picked me up

Turned me around

How he placed my feet on solid ground

It makes me wanna shout

Hallelujah

Thank you Jesus

Lord you're worthy

Of all the glory

And all the honour

And all the praise

As I sang those songs I didn't know what was happening to my heart. I felt as though I was really singing them to Jesus and really thanking him. As I sang I thought about how sick I had been, how much I had carried around and had tried to figure out. Since my recovery, right up to this day, I had been searching for something, something that I couldn't quite put my finger on. As I sang those songs I began to feel my heart softening and filling up.

I don't remember what the pastor spoke about, but I do remember that he asked everyone to stand once he had finished. He asked whether there was anyone in the hall who wanted to give their lives to Jesus Christ. He spoke for a few minutes about this and while he was speaking I began to speak to God. That particular Sunday was my birthday and as I spoke to God I remembered how I had made my own agreement with Him when I was in the hospital: "I promised you I would come to church if I survived the surgery. Sorry I've taken so long. You saved my life, now it's time to give to you what you gave back to me."

The pastor asked people to come to the front of the hall if they would like him to pray for them. I don't remember walking to the front, but I did somehow. I repeated a prayer and then I heard a lot of people clapping. Afterwards I went to a room with two smiley young women called Genevieve and Samantha. They explained in more detail about what salvation was and asked if they could have my number so that they could keep in touch.

I gave them my details and Genevieve mentioned in conversation that prayer took place in the church office every morning during the week. I began to ask about where that was located and what time it took place and before I knew it I had a date with Genevieve for 6 am the following day.

I continued to attend prayer meetings, new believers' classes and the home group that Genevieve held at her house. Genevieve became my spiritual mother and taught me a lot, took me to conferences, seminars and to retreats. It was a great time of developing my relationship with Jesus, with others and growing more into the person that God had created me to be.

Before I knew it a few months had gone by and so much seemed to have happened. I no longer felt anxious, depressed, lost or alone. I seemed to have overcome all of those things and not even realised it was happening! I assumed that was because I was busy with many new things.

As the year came around I felt like a different person in relation to all my baggage. I felt lighter, I no longer felt burdened as though I was carrying the weight of the world on my shoulders. I learned how to pray, learned and practised fasting and continued to study the Bible. The different Bible study classes that the church had during the week helped me to understand the scriptures a bit more than before.

I had received the gift of the Holy Spirit after a few months of giving my life to Jesus. This really helped my prayer life and I began to have dreams and know things about people that were not public knowledge. As I continued learning about the gifts of the Holy Spirit I realised that I was receiving words of knowledge about others through the Holy Spirit. The more I spoke to God, the more I spent time studying the Bible and fasting, the closer I felt to Him and the less I focused on me. I didn't think that could ever have been possible, but it was the change of focus that brought a change in my heart and in my life.

CHAPTER NINE

The Plans He Has for Us

The last thing on my mind was dating. I was learning about God and that was the only relationship I was interested in. I was learning to trust Him, learning to love Him and learning about His love for me. He seemed to have my best interests at heart. My new relationship with God didn't really leave room for anyone else, as I just wanted to spend my hours getting to know more about Him. I've learned over the years that we may have our plans, but God also has His and it is His purpose that prevails. During the period of June 2003 and September 2003 he brought a suitor for me in the form of Jean-Marc. Yes, the guy I sat next to when I first went to church. I then realised that God had a sense of humour. I learned that my cousin Nickelas had invited him to church, had mentored him and that Jean-Marc had started going to church in May 2003, a month before me. Nothing was a coincidence.

However, a Christian relationship seemed alien to me. I was told and heard pastors preaching in services about saving yourself (not having sex before marriage), and the reasons for doing so. I was told that the teachings were in line with God's word in the Bible, so, of course, I did my homework. I found that it did say in the Bible that it was better to marry than burn. I wondered whether it meant burn in hell for committing some kind of sin, or burn from the desire to be doing something else? So I began to seek answers. As I began to study my understanding was that if one couldn't control their sexual desires, if they were burning with passion and finding it hard to control their sexual desires outside of marriage, that it would be a good idea for them to get married. It seemed that to have sexual relations outside of marriage was unacceptable. If I was following the word of God and taking Christianity seriously, then it meant I would also need to follow not some of what the bible said, but all of it.

I concluded that celibacy wasn't a problem to me because I still wasn't settled about the marriage thing.

The people that I had observed who were in relationships within the church seemed seriously involved; the idea of a fling probably had never entered their minds. Their attitude to a relationship reminded me of thoughts I had as a teenager before I really knew anything about boys. These Christians seemed so pure and innocent – the opposite of me! This further confirmed in my mind that marriage, especially Christian marriage, was for others and definitely not for me. Marriage seemed like such a major commitment at any age, but even more so for the Christians that I knew who were about to take that step.

I wondered if they knew what they were getting themselves into.

Marriage wasn't always the romantic idyll that Hollywood depicted! I had never really been interested in marriage because of the experiences that I'd had and the things that I had seen over the years. Marriage seemed like something that, in this day and age, people didn't really understand and value, so to me it wasn't worth getting into. But in the church, women seemed to look forward to the day when they would get married and it was a major topic of conversation. I found this quite disturbing.

I became nervous when asked the recurring question, "Are you dating?" It was a scary thought to say "Yes", as it seemed that in church if you began dating someone, marriage was soon to follow. I didn't want to get married, because from what I had seen, marriage didn't work. I also wasn't ready to be in a relationship where someone would be so close to me that they would have access to my 'world': there was too much to deal with and too much to explain. So I continued speaking to Jean-Marc and got to know more about him from a distance. Months went by and without even realising it he had become a good friend. Several people asked me what my intentions were towards him, and I couldn't give a clear answer. I knew that I was at the age and stage where I should want to settle down, but whenever I had tried to settle down before it had ended in heartache. The miraculous thing that had also begun to happen over the months of speaking to him was that there were sparks of intrigue in me with regards to marriage. I continued my biblical research on marriage, and it was through the research that I began to find out that marriage was God's idea. God had created marriage for a man to have a suitable helper in the form of a woman, and for them to fulfil their purpose through Him.

It all seemed the opposite of what I had been taught. I had observed that some of the older generation had adhered to these principles, but these ideas seemed old fashioned and to favour the chauvinistic views of some of the men I had come across in the past. But as I read on and studied the Bible, I realised that God had a way of doing things and everything that He did had a reason. If He had stated that the man was to rule over the woman, then I wanted to know the reason for it. There had to be a reason for it – this was God we were talking about!

I began to read the first book of the Bible, Genesis. I reached Chapter 3, and then began to see why God had put things in the order that he had in relation to men and women. I had to read more. It wasn't enough just to read about Adam and Eve; it would take more for me to surrender the title of 'Head of my household' and 'Leader of all in my life'!

I went on to read Chapter 18 of the book of Genesis, and read about Sarah, Abraham's wife. I then read Chapter 16 in the book of Judges, about Samson and an interesting lady called Delilah. I then went on to read the book of Ruth, then in 2 Samuel I read about David and Bathsheba.

I also studied Solomon and his many wives in 1 Kings, Chapter 11. I read the book of Esther and about how the young queen saved a nation, and then read about Abigail and how she saved her husband's honour and life in 1 Samuel, Chapter 25. I continued to read about the women whose stories had been chosen to enlighten the many women who would come after them, and I began to see things a little more clearly. God didn't see women as second class, or second to the man. God had created woman out of man by taking one of Adam's ribs. If God wanted to make woman separate then He probably would have created her the same way as He did Adam, but He didn't do that. God created a helpmate out of the man, someone who was comparable to man. The more I read of the Bible, the more it made me realise that in the examples of the relationships that had coloured my view of marriage so far, both the men and the women had veered away from God's original plan for marriage.

As I began to gain more spiritual insight, my heart began to soften towards the idea of marriage and I even began to have discussions with Jean-Marc. I was still battling with a few thoughts, and remembered watching the film *My Big*

Fat Greek Wedding, and recalled the mother telling her daughter before she was about to embark on the journey of marriage, "Women are the neck that turns the head."

I had heard that expression before, but was still unsure whether that was true. What if you had a husband who was so stubborn and always thought he was right, and on top of that was so prideful that even if he was wrong he would never say sorry? What would happen in a marriage like that? I had seen it many times before: someone had to give and I knew that in the past that person had always been me. I was tired of being walked over and stamped on and that's how I had seen marriage. The woman always seemed to have to give in and give up more than the man. It wasn't fair.

I knew that Jean-Marc was a kind man and even though he was stubborn at times, he was gentle enough for me to be able to handle. Maybe he was the man for me?

I continued in the mode of indecisiveness for about five months. I spent more and more time with Jean-Marc, and in the end he won me over with his sincere and genuine nature. We got engaged in February 2004 and married on the same date that my parents married, the 14th October 2004.

We had much to work out as individuals and in our marriage due to past hurts and much baggage. Jean-Marc was a gentle, laid back character who was consistently calm. I was ... well, you know about me by now so I don't need to begin to explain. I thought it would have been quite straightforward: I would be the organiser and Jean-Marc could fall inline. He wasn't an organiser and admitted so. The reality wasn't like that. I began to see another side to Jean-Marc and I couldn't understand what his problem was.

I really thank God for my many mentors, but in this particular season of life Sheron was a blessing to me. Sheron was our pastor's wife, she had been married for over 10 years, and had been a Christian for even longer than that. There was something in her that I had liked from the moment I met her. She was honest and always managed to get the point across in a practical and funny way. I asked her to mentor me in 2005 and she accepted, which I was pleased about. I hadn't realised what I was letting myself in for, as during one of our one to one sessions she decided it was time to sort me out. I was asked how everything was going with Jean-Marc, and I went off into a rant as usual, complaining about him not doing this, that and the other in the way that I wanted it to be done. After listening intently Sheron looked at me and smiled (with that unique smile she has just before telling you something you may not particularly like), and said, "Marsie, can I ask you, what makes you think that your way is always the right and best way to do things?"

I was stunned because the people around me never questioned my suggestions or order, they just did what I asked or said most of the time. I had never thought there was another way of looking at an issue. My way had always been the best way, and as it was my world that Jean-Marc had stepped into when he moved into the flat, I had expected him to fall into line like everything and everyone usually did. I always organised things in the best way possible, so as far as I was concerned my way was the best way, but she did get me thinking. That was the trigger to many things changing in our marriage. Certain things took longer than others due to the emotional attachments, but the changes happened.

We had been married for three months when Jean-Marc began discussing with me that he was thinking about not completing his final year of university. I was concerned and believed that if he started his degree that he should complete it. It seemed like a better idea in the long-term for his future career, but he wanted to gain practical experience in the film industry. We were living on one salary, as the work from the part-time job that Jean-Marc used to do as a security guard had suddenly dried up. The flat that we lived in was nice, but hardly big enough for the two of us. There was no way that we could afford to move and buy a house in London, and it definitely wasn't the ideal time to have a child.

Jean-Marc always believed that we would have at least two children, but I didn't believe that I would ever conceive because of my medical history. We prayed about having children and believed God revealed to us that we would have a daughter and a son. We prayed about the names and we heard the names Julienne and Jesse. I was overwhelmed and not quite sure how it all would work financially, but we realised that the timing would never be perfect. If God had told us about our children we believed that we were meant to have them, He would provide for us.

It was a day in January 2005 when we both sensed that we ought to try for our first child, Julienne. In February 2005 we took a test as I was feeling more tired than usual and we found out that I was pregnant. I was in shock and then the panic began to set in. I began to think about what type of mother I would be, was I really ready for a child? It was one thing to desire these things, but when it actually happened it was a different ball game. I was going to have a baby, and I knew deep down that life would never be the same again.

When the time came for the scan at 20 weeks, we were booked to have it at St Thomas' hospital in London. I had begun to get used to the idea of being a Mummy, and was enjoying my pregnancy. Jean-Marc came with me to the scan and was very excited about Julienne. We had decided to name the baby Julienne after Jean-Marc's Mum who had passed away some years before. It had been a traumatic time for Jean-Marc, as his Mum was the pillar in their family, but he was slowly getting over things. We had been praying about Julienne from the moment we had heard God speak to us about her. Her name meant 'youthful', and we prayed that she would be playful and joyful.

During the scan the stenographer joked with us and asked us if we would like to know the sex of the baby and we laughed and said we already knew, but he could tell us if he liked. He said to us, "So your guess is it's a girl then?"

Jean-Marc, who is a true man of God smiled and said, "Our God is really great. We know it's a girl".

The stenographer then put the camera in position and turned the screen towards us. "Well we can be 99 per cent sure that it's a girl."

We smiled at one another, as not only was it a great sight to see our baby at 20 weeks with her little limbs, but it was a testimony to God's all-knowing power.

It was then that the stenographer mentioned that Julienne seemed a little low down and he wanted to get a second opinion. A colleague of his came in to view the screen and confirmed it was best to see a doctor before leaving the hospital. Something didn't seem right. I was asked to get dressed, as a doctor needed to perform a physical check-up and I had to wait until he was available. Once the doctor became available he did an internal check and said that Julienne's head was engaged, the cervix was open and she was ready to come, he could feel it. I couldn't believe what was happening, I was only 20 weeks pregnant. The doctor discussed various options with us, stitches and suppositories, and also recommended that I rest. He explained that he wanted me to stay overnight in the hospital for observation, and he would also be recommending that I see one of the consultants. Jean-Marc was with me all the way, he never left my side, but I suggested that he go home and rest as I sensed that the following day could be a long one for him.

A paediatric consultant came to see me the following morning, by which time Jean-Marc had called me to say that he was on his way back to the hospital. I wasn't in pain, but felt heaviness in my lower parts from the weight of Julienne pushing down. I had been praying the night before and had let friends, family and our pastors know about the situation, so that they could be praying alongside us.

The consultant had explained that I needed to have complete bed rest. He was hopeful that we could get past 30 weeks, and if Julienne was born at that stage, she would be stronger, more developed and have a better chance of survival. To be honest at that stage I didn't hear what the consultant said, all I heard from the doctors was that my cervix was open and Julienne was engaged and could come at any moment. I had to rest. In my mind there was no way she was coming early, she would come when she was fully developed and she would be healthy. I had to get home to pray.

I was housebound. I had been stopped in my tracks and had plenty of time to reflect. God was funny. Every time that I was about to make a mess of my life He kindly intervened.

While confined to the house I began to read a book called *Supernatural Childbirth*. I took on board what the author had written about praying the word of God into situations when there may have been complications during pregnancy. I wrote down my battle plan:

"What I believe is this, we'll have nothing less than this; I will go into hospital and have Julienne without pain, without stitches, without anaesthetic, without further complications. I will give birth with joy – expressing joy. Julienne will be born whole, healthy and a child belonging to God."

Apart from the two stitches I had to have due to Julienne pointing her finger as she was delivered (like mother like daughter), all of the above came to pass and Julienne was born five days early. In the end, Julienne was a full-term baby. Yet again, I had to thank God for His faithfulness.

Things were still strained in the marriage department, but because I was forced to take a back seat regarding decision-making during pregnancy, Jean-Marc was able to get on with organising our life and make the life-changing decisions that were necessary for us to progress as a family. One of the major decisions was a move to Kent. I had lived in London for 15 years, almost as long as I had lived in Yorkshire, and it was home for me. The change of scenery and the idea of having to create a new social network were daunting. I had always said that I didn't want to raise children in London, and Jean-Marc having been raised in Paris was fed up with city life. I was actually tired of London and fancied leaving England altogether, but it was a bit late for that. We sold the flat, moved to Kent and had a new baby all within a month. It was a lot of change, but Jean-Marc and I had made the decision for our family. As time went on Jean-Marc and I still had our power struggles, but I found that motherhood had begun to soften me.

Julienne was growing more and more each day, and it was time for me to return to work. It was hard leaving Julienne, but at the same time it was great to go back to work as I missed the interaction with adults. Jean-Marc had begun to work in a self-employed capacity and after a few months of being back at work I discussed with Jean-Marc whether we ought to begin praying into when to try for Jesse. We prayed and asked God about the timing and we sensed we had the go-ahead. Jesse was conceived in November 2006. When we had prayed about Jesse, we sensed he would be a handful for many different reasons … little did we know.

I had been back at work about six months when we found out that I was pregnant again. We hadn't thought about the logistics, we had just been focused on what we believed God had told us, that it was time for Jesse to be born. As I thought about breaking the news to my managers, I realised that more maternity leave might be a problem for them. I had returned to work in August 2006, and would be due to go off on maternity leave again in August 2007. Surprisingly when I told them they were fine. They mentioned how it would affect the rota, but on the whole they were really pleased and that was a relief. I was enjoying my time at work. I had gone back on a part-time basis and only worked two days per week. It was a perfect balance, as I didn't want to overdo it.

We were renting accommodation and the landlord decided to sell the property we were living in. He gave us ample notice, but the move date just happened to coincide with the second trimester of my pregnancy. Jean-Marc was working full-time by then and was busy most days at work, but I was feeling great during those months so felt capable of coping with another house move. The complications with Julienne were out of my mind as I was already in my 25th week of pregnancy and felt great. We had significant help during the move, but there were things to do like cleaning both houses and preparing them at either end.

We collected the keys for the new house on the 16th June 2007, and then I started the task of getting the house in order before we moved in. I was between the two houses doing bits and pieces, working to get the jobs done, taking care of Julienne who was a toddler at that stage, working part-time and doing all of the other bits and pieces that I decided to get involved in. I went to work on the 19th June 2007 and, feeling quite tired, went to lie down in one of the rest pods during the morning of my 10 am–8 pm shift. My boss said I could rest up until my lunch hour and then go back to cover the desk from 3.30 pm onwards. I rested from 11 am up until 2 pm, woke up and had a shower to freshen up. I went back to the reception room, ate lunch and had a chat with the girls until it was time to go back to work.

I decided to visit the ladies before heading back to the desk, and it was then that something felt a bit strange. As I was refastening my trousers water began to trickle down the inside of my thigh. I wondered what was happening. I was six months pregnant – the last thing on my mind was that it could have been my waters breaking. My impression of waters breaking was gleaned from films, when the event is often quite dramatic. My waters hadn't broken with Julienne, so I didn't have a clue what was happening now.

I went back to the reception room and tried to call one of my colleagues who had given birth before, as I thought she might have known what was going on. I couldn't get hold of her so I called my team leader to explain why I wasn't back on the desk, as it was past 3.30 pm. My team leader listened intently as I explained calmly what had happened, she then said, "I'm coming in."

My manager, who was three floors away on the other side of the building had also been informed and managed to make it to the reception room about a second after my team leader did. I was now on the phone to Dartford hospital and they informed me that I should go to the hospital closest to my work place, which was St Thomas'. If Jesse was coming this early they would have to send me back to St Thomas' anyway as they didn't have a baby unit at Dartford for premature babies less than 30 weeks. In my mind Jesse wasn't coming early, there was no need to panic as we'd been here before.

We made it to St Thomas' hospital and had to go through the process of a midwife checking to see whether I really needed to be there. Jean-Marc arrived frantically about half an hour later, as it was his day to pick Julienne up from our child minder. I was taken care of and admitted to the hospital by a lovely midwife called Teresa Kenny on Tuesday 19th June 2007, and by Saturday 23rd June 2007 Jesse entered the world weighing just 710 grams. Mum said when we announced Jesse's birth, "Not even a bag of sugar."

He was wrapped in a bag and taken away to the neonatal unit as soon as I gave birth, I didn't have the chance to hold him.

I didn't believe that Jesse would be born early. I had prayed for him in the same manner that I had prayed for Julienne when we had faced a similar hurdle, but he arrived 3 months early anyway.

People joked that he was too inquisitive and wanted to know what was going on outside, and that he thought he was grown enough to come out and survive in the world. When I saw him for the first time in the evening after giving birth I was shocked and cried my heart out.

Throughout the pregnancy Jean-Marc had told me to slow down, take it easy and rest. I felt great, and decided to go against everything Jean-Marc was telling me to do, and Jesse came early. When I saw him lying there in such a fragile state, I blamed myself. Why couldn't I just listen for once? Why did I always think that I knew best? I realised that it wasn't about me anymore; parenting was about them, those little ones whose lives depended upon me. It was then that my attitude began to change towards many things.

Jesse was in three different hospitals over a period of two months. It was a time in my life that seemed to stand still. Every gram Jesse gained in weight meant he was closer to coming home. Every wire that was taken away meant he was progressing. Every piece of clothing that was removed meant that the systems of his body were beginning to work for themselves.

The church was praying, we were praying, people that we didn't even know were praying, as they had heard the story about Jesse through different sources, and it touched them.

But as ever, God made all of the different situations work together for a good reason. Jean-Marc and I became closer, the struggles for power ceased and we became united in battle. We realised we had a family and whatever it took for us to work together we would do it to ensure that we kept what God had given us.

Jesse came home when he was 36 weeks old, weighing three pounds.

I had such peace about Jesse's situation and was thankful that we had become closer as a family.

Life seemed to be moving on, the children were growing up quickly and I was back at work full time. All seemed to be going well and then we were hit with another bombshell. Mum was diagnosed with lung cancer. It was March 2012, but Mum hadn't been feeling well for about two years prior to that. The doctors had done various tests but had always come back with the same answer – all clear. They couldn't seem to find anything wrong. The cough that she had lived with for years got worse and just wouldn't go away and this was diagnosed as asthma; the pains in her legs were put down to arthritis.

Mum was well known for her candid approach, which she somehow seemed to express regardless of the circumstances or the stature of the person she was speaking to. Every time she visited her doctor she would tell him that he didn't know what he was doing and that instead of sending her for all of these silly tests, he needed to test her for cancer. He would say to her that he didn't think she had cancer and he would try some other test. The one thing that we all used to say about Mum was that if she said anything or picked up on anything, we ought to take note, as she would say things and often, either weeks or months later, they would happen.

This time, sadly she foresaw what would eventually take her to her grave. I had been to Yorkshire to help to take care of Mum as she had begun to suffer from major pain, especially at night. My sister and nieces were tired as they had been taking care of her leading up to that point and I had to try and do my part. I didn't realise how precious that time was with Mum, as it was the last time I would be able to fully converse properly with her face to face.

We talked about the past, how she was feeling, and what she expected all of us to do when she passed away. Mum apologised for only being half a mother, as we spoke of things that had happened in the past. I knew she was referring to her bouts of drinking and the outbursts that ensued. I had seen many things as I became older and realised that Mum did the best she could with the knowledge she had. Her parents had never really loved her unconditionally, and when she married dad she poured everything into him and her children. When they split up the only thing she had left were her children. Her ideal picture, of being married and raising a family together, was no longer intact. Her heart was broken and she didn't know how to get back up from the blow … so she began to drink.

There was a stage in my life where the drinking and all of the crazy outbursts that came with it were embarrassing. But it then got to the stage where I saw Mum before she would drink and then after, and realised I was seeing two different people. The Mum before alcohol was wise, witty and dependable and the Mum after alcohol was just the opposite. I saw what the spirit of addiction could do and knew that it could be very destructive to all involved. But despite the trials and challenges we faced as a family, I had forgiven Mum and loved her so much … she was definitely more than half a mother!

Perhaps this is a West Indian thing, but even before anything was ever wrong with Mum she spoke very openly about her death and how she wanted things to be. The sentence in patois would be,

"When mi dead … ". It was always followed by a list of instructions: the casket she wanted, the clothes she wanted to wear, how her hair should look, where she wanted to be buried, and a host of other details. Over the years we had heard all of this, and the list often ended with the threat, An mi wi cum bak an tickle yu foot bottom if you nu du we mi se." She would always laugh as she threatened to come back to tickle our feet if we were disobedient. The one thing that I can say about Mum was that she was a bit of a comedian.

On my return from Yorkshire I felt extremely tired, but didn't think anything of it and assumed that it was just over tiredness due to the fact that I had been up with Mum throughout the night. Mum couldn't sleep due to the pain and extreme perspiration she was suffering from, and I barely slept as I needed to change her sheets, wipe her down constantly and try and comfort her, as she would cry out in pain. The pain relief didn't really help at that stage and it was so hard to see her in such a degenerated state, but I had to be strong. I made her food and cleaned and tidied up during the day and would have a baby monitor in my room at night to keep an ear open for her. So, I just put the tiredness down to not having sleep for a few days. But as the week went on I didn't seem to be recovering, so we decided to do a pregnancy test and it was positive. We were happy, but the timing for me left me hugely concerned. How was I going to look after Mum, what was going to happen to her? We went to the doctors to double check, and it was true, we were expecting our third baby. I just didn't know how I was going to break the news to Mum.

A few days later I started losing blood and I recognised the signs as it had happened before during my previous pregnancies. This time I didn't want to take any unnecessary risks, as this was our third child and I was almost 40. I had been lifting Mum when I was in Yorkshire, as she no longer had the strength to move herself to sit up in bed. We needed to keep her upright as she was coughing, and when she coughed it resonated through her whole body and caused her extreme pain … and that was when she would cry out. Lifting Mum hadn't helped, and I realised that it probably brought the complications of the pregnancy on much sooner.

I was at work when I began to have stomach cramps and the bleeding began to increase. Jean-Marc was working in the same office as me at the time, so this time around it was easy to locate him. I made all of the necessary arrangements to leave the office that day, and as we awaited the arrival of the taxi Jean-Marc and I silently prayed that God would keep our baby.

After going through the procedures at Darenth Valley Hospital we were assigned to a very capable consultant called Gabriel Awadzi. I knew from the moment I met Him that God had sent him to take care of us and to ensure our baby would be fine. I found it so 'God' that our consultant would be named Gabriel, who in the Bible was an angel who would bring messages from God for specific people. I didn't believe in coincidence and knew that it was God's way of encouraging us and helping us to be at peace knowing that He was in control of everything.

As the weeks passed by my cervix began to open. This was familiar territory but was happening slightly earlier on in this pregnancy than with Julienne. Bed rest for the remainder of the pregnancy was recommended, as well as appointments every two weeks to measure the cervix. It was a trying time, more so because I couldn't travel anywhere, which meant I couldn't go to Yorkshire to see Mum. I spoke to my sister or nieces every day, and I could hear how tired they were and how difficult it was becoming for them watching as Mum's health deteriorated. I would try and speak to Mum, but sometimes she was sleeping; if not asleep she was too tired to talk and at other times she just didn't want to speak to me. When we broke the news to Mum that I was pregnant she fell silent, then asked why two children weren't enough. I had to point out to her that she had had five children, but then she explained her fears for me: the last two pregnancies were hard, so why would I want to have another one? I remember Mum saying to me that at my age I had been through enough, and if she had to go through what I had been through she wouldn't have been able to do it. I assured her that she would, because it's amazing how resilient we are as human beings … and she, in particular, was a fighter. I thought Mum was scared of losing me, that she was afraid that something bad was going to happen. I reassured her that God had it all under control and all she said to that was, "Mmm, does he now." Typical Mum.

As time went on and Mum became bedridden she told me she felt abandoned by me, and that she expected me out of all of her children to be there to take care of her when she was ill. I was devastated. I was in bed, not even able to walk up and down the stairs once a day without feeling as though our baby was going to be born, and on top of this Mum was dying about 200 miles away in Yorkshire and I was not able to take care of her. I felt as though I was being put in a position where I had to choose one life over another, and it was one of the most distressing positions I'd ever been in.

Our baby was due to be born on New Year's Eve. It seemed like an unending time to be on bed rest. There were so many things that were meant to happen in the coming months. The most important thing was Mum's 70th because even though I didn't want to admit it, I sensed it would be the last time we celebrated her birthday. There was also my 40 birthday, our wedding anniversary, my sibling's birthdays, Julienne's birthday and then, of course, Christmas. It made me realise all the more that we never know what is around the corner. I read in the Bible that there are many plans in a man's heart, but it's God's purpose that prevails. We plan as men but do not know what tomorrow is going to bring. I could see that those words were proving themselves to be true in my life.

The Macmillan team would visit Mum on a regular basis, and if I had any particular questions or they were considering different types of pain relief I would speak to them. They were absolutely phenomenal and cared for Mum fantastically. It was during October 2012 that they informed me that it wouldn't be long before Mum passed away, and that if I wanted to see her before that happened it would be best to try and make my way to Yorkshire.

My cervix was still open, but if I restricted movement the measurements remained the same. If I walked up and down the stairs in the house, for example, my cervix would open a few millimetres. It didn't sound like much, but as our baby got heavier over the weeks that also put pressure on the cervix and was causing it to open at a faster rate. I needed to minimise my movements as much as possible so that I wouldn't go into labour.

When I received the news about Mum I was due to see my consultant a few days later. I hadn't told him about my Mum as there was no need, but I knew that the time had come for discussion, as I needed to travel to Mum. I wanted to ask his advice about the best way to go about making the journey without endangering our baby.

When I entered the consulting room Mr Awadzi was as jovial as usual. He was a huge formula one fan, so I would normally talk to him about his passion as he did all of his checks. After he finished all of the internal checks and was happy with what he observed he would turn the screen towards me and explain any changes. On that particular week he was very pleased with what he had observed. The measurements of the cervix were the same as the previous week. Measurements of the baby were taken and showed good growth and we could see that the heart was beating well. We just needed to keep doing what we were doing. He was so pleased that we had made it to 30 weeks, as when we had first met I was about 12 weeks pregnant and very anxious about losing our baby. It was now a total contrast and I thanked God each day for keeping both the baby and I in good health and giving us peace throughout. I began to explain to Mr Awadzi that I needed to travel to Yorkshire over the weekend and the reason for it. I could see the shock on his face as I explained that my Mum was critically ill, that she had lung cancer and was in the final stages of life. If we wanted to see her before she passed away it we had been advised that it was best to start to make arrangements to see her as soon as possible.

Mr Awadzi was so lovely and mentioned that he had very similar circumstances a few years before, and it was never easy. He was amazed under the circumstances how I had remained so positive and calm and recommended that I have steroid injections to help the development of the baby's lungs before travelling. He also asked where in Yorkshire I would be staying and recommended that if I were to go into labour that I go to Sheffield Hallam hospital as they would be able to deliver and care for the baby there. That was perfect, as we had planned to stay with Wayne and Elaine and they were still living in Sheffield.

He arranged my appointment for the steroid injection and wished me luck, it was as though he didn't expect to see me again. I continued to pray and look to God. The things that I had found helped me immensely during each complicated pregnancy were peace, patience and prayer. I learned to listen to my husband and most importantly to stand on the word of God and have faith in what He said he would do.

I would always pray a lot before going to hospital appointments as I found that if I didn't I would come out of the consultancy room anxious, overwhelmed and fearing the worst. When we found out that my cervix was open during my pregnancy with Julienne, I remember calling my cousin Karen while waiting at the hospital pharmacy with Jean-Marc. Jean-Marc and I had both been born again Christians for about two years, so were still baby Christians in certain respects, but were facing the trial of being told by the doctor that the baby could be born at 20 weeks, at which stage of prematurity, there was a high risk that her life may not be preserved. When I told Karen what the doctors said she encouraged me and said;

"Mars, the doctors are professionals and they go by what they see and give their report. What we do is use the information from that report and bring it to God in prayer. We pray until what you want to see, until what God has promised concerning your baby comes to pass. Remember, we go by God's report as God is in control".

When I came off the phone to Karen my viewpoint had changed. The Lord had spoken to Jean-Marc and I clearly about Julienne, and why would he do that if she would die? That didn't make sense to me at all, but what did make sense was that in order for her to live and be born healthy and whole I needed to pray. I prayed about everything that God had promised us regarding our daughter until the day she was born full term and I held her in my arms!

What I learned during that pregnancy was that as human beings we tend to draw upon what we learn from our exposure and experiences, from our times of desperate need.

I managed to see Mum two weeks before she passed away. My main concern was that she hadn't given her life to the Lord and where she would end up if she didn't. Mum had suffered long enough on this earth and the last thing I wanted was her suffering for the rest of eternity. Jean-Marc and I had the opportunity to speak to Mum alone while she was taking her afternoon rest in bed. We spoke to her about giving her life to the Lord and she just smiled. Jean-Marc asked her if she wanted to give her life to Him and she nodded her head to say yes. We held her hands and Jean-Marc prayed for her and led Mum to the Lord, it was really beautiful, we were so happy.

Afterwards we spoke to Mum about heaven and read scriptures to encourage her about where she would be going as she said that she would be scared to meet Jesus. We assured her and by the time we finished she was smiling and saying to us that she could see streets of gold and hear bells ringing, she also mentioned the singing, lots of singing she said. We knew she was ready to go.

Mum went to be with the Lord on Sunday 11 November 2012. I cried, because as my aunt said to me, "Because we come from our Mothers, when they go it's as though a part of us leaves too".

That was the best explanation anyone gave for the way I felt at the very moment that I received the news of her death from my niece over the phone. "She's gone, aunty, she's gone now".

Mum passing was always going to be difficult, but the other thing to deal with was seeing my uncle. I had spoken to my Mum about the abuse before she passed away. I had told my brother Wayne and I thought it was too much to expect him to carry such a load by himself, and he suggested that I tell Mum. I begged them not to tell my brother Dave, as I knew his temper would have got the better of him and I don't know what he would have done to my uncle if he had found out. We had kept it a secret, just between the three of us. I could see the pain on their faces when we discussed it and I really didn't want to cause more pain and discord to the family, so it was best not to discuss it further. But Mum was now gone. The link to my uncle was gone and I had no reason to be quiet about the whole thing anymore.

I was always concerned about how it would affect Mum and how people would view her and whether she would begin drinking again under the pressure of it all. I knew she felt bad for leaving me exposed, for not protecting me and keeping me safe, and I didn't want to add to her pain.

I had realised as the years had gone by that God had healed me from the abuse. I had been to courses and read books regarding healing and deliverance, especially related to sexual abuse, but it was hard to know whether these things actually worked until confronted with the situation that caused all of the pain in the first place. That confrontation took place soon after my Mum's death.

In West Indian culture it is normal for people to visit the home of the deceased so that what is called "nine nights" can take place. In our case it was more like 19 nights, as from the day that Mum passed away people began to visit to give their condolences. It was a time where sad and happy memories were shared by family and friends, as well as lots of food and strong beverages. It was tiring, but lovely for the people who knew Mum to share the burden and grief of their loss.

I knew that this would be the time that I would see my uncle, as, culturally, he was expected to visit and pay his respects before the day of the funeral.

I didn't know how to feel and I didn't know how I would react. I didn't speak to Jean-Marc or anyone else about it, I just asked God to help me and prepare me for when I saw him, and He did.

I was sitting in the living room of my Mum's house and there were people visiting constantly. When the door of the living room opened I didn't look up as I thought it was someone coming in from the kitchen, as I hadn't heard the front door open or close. My sister was in the living room with me, and when she greeted the person entering my heart leapt for a moment ... it was him! I had secretly hoped that I wouldn't see him until the day of the funeral, in a crowded situation and from a distance, not in the house where he'd abused me and in such close proximity. But as I looked up I saw a man who was ashamed and couldn't even look me in my eyes. Heavily pregnant, I couldn't really stand up easily, so remained seated. He greeted me casually, "Hiya stranger, long time no see."

It had purposely been a long time. I greeted him politely and cordially. As he spoke to my sister I observed him. It had taken him over a week to visit us, which was unusual for close family members. I wondered whether it was because he knew he was going to see me. Was he scared now Mum had passed away that I would expose him to the rest of the family? I sat there with all of these thoughts running through my mind and as I watched him I felt pity for him. Yes, pity. I realised that I was no longer afraid of him and that I had forgiven him. I saw that he probably did what he did because of insecurities and lack of self-worth, and because he had never got caught, he continued. His life wasn't great, his marriage had fallen apart and he looked old. All I wanted to do was to pray for him, as I knew only God could help him.

I realised that the enemy had tried to destroy my life, but the assignment that he had used to try and destroy me had not succeeded. The very one he had sent to destroy me was being destroyed. It was yet another testimony of God's unfailing love and faithfulness towards me. I was able to look at my abuser with compassion and not condemnation.

I didn't think the day would have ever come when I would be inches away from my abuser and be at peace, but it did. There was no need to take it any further as, for me, the chapter was closed and it was a new beginning. I knew I had been healed and delivered and God had helped me as I asked Him to.

When one life is lost, another is given. Our beautiful son Alexander Nehemiah Noah was born approximately six weeks later on Christmas Day. He was born full term, whole and gorgeous. He was God's gift to us, especially to me to bring me joy in a time when God knew I would need it. I thanked God for knowing what was ahead and preparing everything even before we realised what we would need.

With each situation Jean-Marc and I went through together I realised more and more that my husband could be relied upon, and I began to trust him. The more we went through together and the more we worked as a team, the stronger we became. We had our moments and it was easy to slip back into old ways, especially when the pressure was on, but God truly gave us grace. We constantly reminded ourselves that God had put us together for life. We could either work at improving our marriage, or we could leave things undone and unsaid and wait for things to crumble We wanted our marriage to work, so we began to face our demons.

Each day brings a new challenge, but God knows why He made Jean-Marc to be my husband. I can honestly say that I don't think that any other man could be what Jean-Marc is to me – he is a special gift from God to me. As we spend more time together, we learn to understand one another more. We are conscious of how far we have come, and continue to try to put into practice what we have learned. We are still learning a lot and have a lifetime together to keep enjoying each other and working one another out, we truly thank God for that!

The years have passed swiftly since 2001 and my life has done a 360-degree turn. I went through many things in my life that caused me to wonder "Why me?" Before, I would ask myself if there was a God, how could He allow me to go through the pain that I went through? Now, I know He has a plan and a purpose for my life, and He takes what was meant for evil and makes it work for good.

My experiences were tough to go through and at times I wanted to end my life, but there was a bigger plan for my tough times, and knowing Jesus was the beginning. God always amazes me; tears are streaming down my face as I write this because I love God so much. I don't know what I would do without Him.

I didn't think that I was good enough for so many different reasons, but I have learned that there was always a bigger plan and purpose that I couldn't see. The experiences built my character and enabled me to gain a diploma from the University of Life, and I hope that I am wiser because I have overcome certain life experiences. I used to think that life should be straightforward and all about fun, but the reality is that it's not always like that; people get abused, develop cancer, have alcoholics for mothers, absent fathers and much more, but it's our attitude and the choices that we make going forward that will determine where we end up.

The different things that I went through didn't kill me and I thank God for that. I am thankful for every experience I've been through so far, it may sound crazy, but I am. The experiences have helped me to know my true self. They have taught me to forgive, to trust and to love.

In a way I have ended up back where I began. I tried to run from the truth, but only the truth could set me free. It was only when I was able to bring these things out into the open and talk about them that I was able to be truly free from them. While I was silent and they were hidden they held me captive.

Now I am free from poverty (remember, it's a frame of mind, not just about money), free from shame, free from inadequacy, free from abandonment, free from rejection, free from fear of what others think, free from anxiety, free from disease and free from death. I feel lighter. I no longer have to carry the weight of the world around, and now the truth is out in the open there is nothing to hold me back. I carried many secrets around for such a long time and they caused all sorts of problems: mental, physical and spiritual, as you have read. Now I can see, the veil has been removed from my eyes and I know that there was no need to let the devil and his entourage have access to my life to harass me.

I was seeking love and happiness in the wrong places, running away to foreign destinations trying to find peace. God never forced me but waited patiently, knowing that I would try His way in the end. The love that I longed for and never really had, God gave to me first through knowing Him. His love doesn't have conditions or constraints. He just loves me unconditionally.

The journey that I have written about began many years ago, but the last seven years have truly been a time of acceptance and revelation, acceptance of myself, acceptance of situations, and the revelation of who God is to me. It has taken many years to complete this book because it has been a therapeutic medium of expression as healing and restoration has taken place for me. It has been a great help to meditate on and gain wisdom from the many lessons that life has taught me so far.

I had my challenges, doubts and insecurities but I was committed to being obedient to what I felt the Lord had asked me to do, which was to write a book that was whispered into my heart by Him, that would touch the hearts and lives of those who chose to read it.

I have been shown that trust begins with a decision and continues to be a choice. I've done what I was asked to do and it has been a journey within itself, but God has begun the work that I have allowed and now I am on the road to being who He has truly created me to be.

I am now in a place where I can freely share with others what God has done for me, and I can do it without apprehension. God is real, and I believe that He has a plan and purpose for every one of our lives. He has even written it in His special book of life for us – the Bible. I also know that He can only help us if we allow Him to, we all need Him regardless. I was messed up. I'm still a work in progress that will never be perfect until Jesus returns and I give Him thanks daily for His grace and mercy towards me.

My hope my prayer, is that this will not be just another book for you. I pray that all of the pictures, words and emotions that have been conjured up within you as you have been reading this book have set you on a journey. I will also be praying that you won't run away, but that you will draw near to Him as He draws near to you, and He whispers truth into your heart.

If you would like to know Jesus more, you can say the following prayer:

"Lord, I recognise that I have been living for myself and not for You up until now and I want you to change that. I want and need you in my life. I acknowledge that you died on the cross for my redemption, and I want to receive the forgiveness that is freely available to me through this sacrifice. Come into my life, Lord, take up residence in my heart and be my Lord and my saviour. I will no longer be controlled by sin, or the desire to please myself, but I will follow you for the rest of my life. My life is now in your hands. I ask this in the wonderful and holy name of Jesus. Amen."

HELPFUL ORGANISATIONS

Below are details of some of the charities/organisations that have helped me over the years. You may also find them useful:

Christian Life Fellowship (CLF) **www.clfi.org.uk**

A non-denominational church firmly rooted in and guided by biblical teachings.

Ellel Ministries www.ellel.org/uk

A non-denominational Christian mission organisation with a vision to welcome people, teach them about the Kingdom of God and heal those in need.

International Christian Women's Network (ICWN) **www.icwn.org.uk**

A Christian charity dedicated to promoting freedom and transformation in the lives of underprivileged and entrapped women around the world.

The Priory www.priorygroup.com

Specialist psychological support and treatment.

Printed in Great Britain
by Amazon

20684169R00098